All proceeds from this book will be donated to the Children's Hospital of Richmond at VCU. Building legacies is important. Building the future of our youth, however possible, is essential.

SECTION 1031 EXCHANGES:

How to Swap Till Ya' Drop, Building Family Wealth While Minimizing Taxes

By Louis J. Rogers

DAVRO PRESS

This edition first published in May 2025 by Davro Press.

ISBN 978-1-7344524-8-8

Cover design by Howard Grossman
Interior design by Leslie Saunderlin

Davro Press

DavroPress.com

Table of Contents:

A Note from the Author

This book is written for real estate owners and operators–regular folks. I apologize in advance to any tax professionals who read the book and say that I have generalized or glossed over some of the more esoteric topics. This is intentional. In the interest of making the book interesting, I aimed to hit the highlights and focus on the most common scenarios, leaving overly complex topics to tax lawyers and CPAs who specialize in real estate taxation.

There are a number of treatises on Section 1031 exchanges designed for practitioners. I have found the *Tax Management Portfolio* series published by Bloomberg Law to be the best source for clear explanation and technical analysis. For this resource, see Levine and Gaynor's *Tax-Free Exchanges Under Section 1031* (Portfolio 567). Also, for a deep dive into Section 1031, see Bradley T. Borden's *Tax-Free Like Kind Exchanges* (3rd edition).

Dedication

This book is dedicated to the many real estate professionals who live in the trenches, structuring, operating, and managing Capital Square's real estate, and to the families who sacrifice so that they can dedicate their professional lives to our investors. Without these hard-working people, it would not be possible to achieve superior returns for thousands of investors across the nation.

Also, this book is dedicated to Doug Britton, a scholar, friend, and the best buddy a UVA sports fan could ever have. Rest in peace, old friend.

Foreword

This book on 1031 exchange investing is written by Louis J. Rogers, one of the true modern innovators in this field. While 1031 investing has been around for over 100 years, Louis has been part of bringing it into modern real estate investing, and he describes this evolution in an easy-to-read style targeted for real estate investors.

The book describes the history of 1031 exchanges, the strengths and weaknesses of various strategies, and compares it with alternative investing strategies. He notes that a "swap till ya' drop" approach can maximize returns. After four hours of reading, you will grasp the essentials with which to knowledgeably interact with a qualified manager to evaluate exchange investing (including Opportunity Zones).

The Delaware Statutory Trust (DST), in whose creation Louis played a key role, is the current state of the art for exchange investing. While this is a highly technical and nuanced structure, this book strips it down to its essentials. This allows the reader to grasp the fundamentals without their eyes glazing over with tax code mumbo jumbo. I have read about this structure many times before, but I found myself learning with each paragraph due to the clarity of exposition.

This book is a must read for anyone considering an exchange as part of their real estate investing activities. I highly recommend this book and will use it as a reference book for years to come.

– Peter Linneman, PhD

Introduction

One of our California investors stopped by Capital Square's Virginia headquarters the other day to visit with us, and he reminded me of his real estate story. He said that when he was a young boy, he had a paper route delivering newspapers. You probably don't know what they are, newspapers. Those were paper things people used to read. Now, they come electronically on your smartphone.

He saved up over years and years and, in 1959, gathered up all his paper route money and bought a small rental house in California. Imagine that: he rolled up his paper route money into a rental house, and that rental house was transformed over time into a large net worth. How? He became a serial exchanger, exchanging over and over again for many decades. A single-family rental house exchanged for a duplex. Then the duplex exchanged for a quad and then for a small apartment building–all in California.

After many decades, when he was tired of the three T's –tenants, toilets, and trash–that come with property management, he decided to sell again. And, once again, rather than paying the taxes, he structured the sale as a Section 1031 tax-deferred exchange. This time, he exchanged for a fractional interest in several large apartment communities in the Southeast. Instead of buying another "whole" property in California that he had to manage, he invested in a Delaware statutory trust (DST), which is a fractional interest in real estate that qualifies for tax deferral under Section 1031. By using the DST structure, he reduced his risk from a concentrated investment in a single property to a more diversified investment in several investment-grade apartment communities throughout the Southeast that provide tax-sheltered income plus tax benefits and potential for appreciation from continued real estate ownership without the hassles of property management. More about DSTs later.

Bottom line: this equation, from a simple rental house to an interest in investment-grade replacement property, provides the road map for superior returns with maximum tax benefits, and this investor has seen it all happen during his lifetime.

Now, there's no more work for him—no more tenants, toilets, and trash—just steady cash flow and appreciation. Capital Square, the real estate firm I founded in 2012, is managing his real estate portfolio composed of seven or eight DST investments that all began with the sale of that rental house purchased from a paper route back in 1959. He says he likes it much better. He's eighty-five years old now and planning his next vacation because he can. He's thrilled to have a national real estate company manage his real estate, relieved to have diversified his holdings outside a single market in California, and enjoys an exceptional retirement without the pain of property management. Multiple 1031 exchanges allowed him to build family wealth and have an incredibly prosperous life. Section 1031, as you will see, can change lives for taxpayers as well as their extended families. Just wait until you hear about my favorite mailman.

We have a clipping of a newspaper article about our paperboy turned investor hanging in the office because it reminds us of how legacies can be built. Hard work transforms outcomes. Smart practices can take that hard work even further.

When I founded Capital Square, I could not have dreamed that my real estate firm would acquire $8 billion of real estate and make the *Inc. 5000* list for eight years in a row, as of the writing of this book. It's a very exciting time around here. It's been a thrilling ride, with many accolades, and I am convinced that the best is yet to come.

I love what I do. If I had to walk to work and pay to be here, I would. Our investors-first firm is my dream come true because it's helping others seize the lives they've always wanted. This book is a guide to tax-advantaged real estate investment solutions because multi-generational legacies are built with knowledge. I hope you will join me on this journey as we have fun with 1031.

Chapter One
Swap Till Ya' Drop

The Essentials

Let's start with a very common scenario of a taxpayer who owns investment real estate. When the time comes to sell, the taxpayer exchanges the property for qualifying replacement property to obtain tax deferral under Section 1031 of the Tax Code. The taxpayer holds the replacement property long term. Upon the taxpayer's death, the taxpayer's heirs receive a step up in tax basis to the then market value of the property. That means the heirs can sell the property free of federal and state income tax, converting tax deferral under Section 1031 into tax forgiveness. This is a strategy used by some of the wealthiest families in the nation, a strategy we commonly refer to as "swap till ya' drop."

The strategy works like this: invest in real estate for the many advantages (for example, cash flow, appreciation, and tax benefits); when the time comes to sell, structure the sale as a tax-deferred exchange under Section 1031; whenever the next time comes to sell the replacement property, exchange over and over again, compounding the value of tax deferral over a lifetime. Because the heirs will inherit the property with a stepped-up tax basis, they can sell the property free of tax (federal and state). In this way, tax deferral under Section 1031 can become tax forgiveness upon death. That is a magical formula for building family wealth.

Note: For large estates, there may be an estate tax.

Terminology

The taxpayer's existing property that is being sold is referred to as the "relinquished property," and the new property to be acquired in the exchange is referred to as the "replacement property."

Tax Deferral: Taxes deferred are not paid currently. They are deferred until the taxpayer sells the replacement property in a taxable transaction. But the smart taxpayer will not sell in a taxable transaction. He or she will instead exchange repeatedly, deferring taxes over and over again, thereby building family wealth without taxation.

Tax Exclusion: The Tax Code provides tax exclusion in several circumstances (for example, the step up in tax basis on death and opportunity zone fund investments that meet certain requirements after a ten-year holding period). This means that the gains are excluded from taxation. In other words, the taxes are forgiven. That is the holy grail of tax planning.

Tax Rates: The taxes deferred in an exchange are composed of:
- Federal depreciation recapture – 25%*
- Federal capital gains – 20% maximum*
- Federal tax on net investment income – 3.8%* (applicable to certain high-income taxpayers)
- State tax – varies from state to state

Section 1031 is my favorite section of the entire Internal Revenue Code. It's over one hundred years old; it's a golden oldie written in simple English: "no gain... shall be recognized." (See Appendix A for the full text.)

We're talking about deferring tax upon the sale of real estate. The mandate, "no gain...shall be recognized," covers property that you have held for investment or used in your business. Take your personal residence out of your mind; it has its own favorable tax provision, but that's a different conversation.

Section 1031 of the Code states: "No gain or loss shall be recognized on the exchange of real property held for productive use in a trade or business or for investment." This relates to investment or business real estate. If you exchange that property for another investment or business property, the tax is deferred. These properties must be of "like kind," and here's where it all began for me.

In the spring of 1984, I finished law school and was offered such an enormous salary of $33,000 that I immediately took a job as a tax lawyer at Hunton & Williams in Richmond, Virginia. That was a lot of money, a tremendous amount of money to me at the time. My exams ended, and on the next Monday, I drove to Main Street in Richmond, Virginia, which was an hour's drive from the University of Virginia in Charlottesville, to begin a new career in taxation.

When I got to work, my new supervisor, who was also a UVA grad, said, "We need you to research Section 1031 exchanges."

I had no idea what he was talking about at the time.

"There's this thing called a like-kind Section 1031 tax-deferred exchange," he continued. "We need to know how it works."

It was my first day on the job, and I was eager to please in my brand-new suit. They sent me into a closet that housed their first computer from Lexus Nexus, a machine as big as a conference table. Its printer paper was perforated with holes running down the sides. Do you remember this? You printed it out and then tore off the perforated edge. So, there I was. This new computer was before me. I was the "young kid" who would understand such a machine. So, I started my research into Section 1031 that has continued to this day.

I went into that closet, and three days later, I came out with the answers. That was the spring of 1984, and here I am four decades later still working on 1031 exchanges. The answers I found remain invaluable, and they can be explained by the single phrase, "swap till ya' drop."

What Hunton & Williams sent me in to discover was how a property can leave an owner's hands, but rather than receiving cash after the sale and paying the taxes, that property instead goes through a 1031 exchange, deferring taxes by acquiring a different property. Basically, if you start with real estate and you end with real estate–and you never receive any cash or non-like-kind property–you've probably done a good exchange. The tax that would have been paid is deferred until you sell the replacement property in a taxable transaction.

This simple process can save a dramatic amount of taxes, both federal and state. As time goes on, you can exchange the replacement property over and over again in a series of exchanges, continually deferring the taxes as your real estate investments appreciate over time. This is how the wealthiest families in the nation build wealth over the decades.

You have the choice at every sale of investment or business property: pay the tax or structure an exchange. You could pay the federal and state taxes, and the tax money is gone. Alternatively, by exchanging, the money that would have been paid in taxes can be reinvested in real estate of your choosing. Then you own the replacement property. It generates income for you, and when it appreciates, you are the beneficiary. Over time, you can easily build a million-dollar net worth in real estate. That is how a boy with a paper route did it and others we'll discuss too.

We call it "swap till ya' drop," because after death, the taxes are no longer deferred. They can be forgiven. If your heirs sell the property, they will do so with a stepped-up tax basis. This means that the heirs can sell without taxation–total tax forgiveness. Imagine the amount of money kept in your family's pocket.

Section 1031 exchanges have had a good hundred-plus-year run. In their 2020 study, "The Tax and Economic Impacts of Section 1031 Like-Kind Exchanges in Real Estate," Professors David C. Ling, PdD, and Milena Petrova, PhD, estimate that 10 to 20% of all commercial real estate transactions involve a Section 1031 exchange.[i] This is an estimate and is likely to result in substantial underreporting of exchanges. Based on my experience, I would estimate the number has been increasing over the years as knowledge about Section 1031 increases and is now closer to 20% to 25%. That is an enormous amount of real estate–billions of dollars of property value and tens of thousands of transactions annually. Repeal of Section 1031 would create a depression in the real estate industry. To prevent such a bad result, the real estate industry has been lobbying Congress for many years in response to suggestions that Section 1031 should be limited or even eliminated entirely. To prove the case, the real estate industry has shown that 1031 creates a large amount of economic activity along with billions of dollars of revenue generated from transactional activity, including local transfer fees, attorney and accounting fees, title insurance costs, and the like.[ii] Several states, such as Florida, Texas, and Nevada, have no income tax, but they still have transfer taxes. If there was no 1031, there'd be dramatically fewer transactions, and many jobs would be lost. Localities would be starved of a large amount of revenue from transfer taxes, and the national economy would be harmed.

This realization has been appreciated by members of Congress. We've gone into their offices and learned how many members of Congress have done 1031 exchanges themselves. I'm hoping that the Code will stand for another hundred years.

Still, back in the day, in 1921 when the predecessor to Section 1031 was adopted, exchanges were very simple. There was a person who had property A, and they swapped with somebody who had property B. Then the first person owned property B and vice versa; it all took place at the same time (a simultaneous exchange). You just swapped properties, nice and simple. If that was the way it remained today, Capital Square probably wouldn't be here (over 350 people would not have jobs with us!) because that kind of property swap doesn't generate a whole lot of excitement. But as it turns out, 1031 became much more exciting over time, starting with the famous *Starker* decision approving a delayed exchange. Don't worry, I'll tell you all about it.

We started with the Internal Revenue Code, which was old school, simple English. Remember, the Internal Revenue Code was once a single volume. You could roll it up and put it in your back pocket while you played golf, if that's your thing. Now, it's several volumes of over 6,800 pages. Today, you'd need a golf cart to carry the Internal Revenue Code, and you'd have no room for your golf clubs.

However, the essence of 1031 remains in the simple language: "no gain…shall be recognized." We're talking about rerouting the gain of what would otherwise be a taxable cash sale to defer the taxes.

Here is how it works.

If you buy an investment or business property and it appreciates, when the time comes to sell, you can exchange it, deferring the federal and state taxes. Now you have a new replacement property. When it matures, you sell it and do another exchange, another exchange, and another exchange. Then, when you meet your maker, your heirs get a stepped-up basis, and they can sell. The taxes (federal and state) will be forgiven. Note: for large estates, there may be an estate tax.

Let's say the taxpayer dies owning a 1031 replacement property with a large, deferred gain (low tax basis plus appreciation). The heirs will be able to sell the inherited replacement property for a market price without taxation. In this way, the deferred tax on inherited 1031 replacement property is excluded from taxation (the tax is forgiven) on death. **Thus, for taxpayers who exchange and own their replacement property at death, the deferral under Section 1031 becomes permanent.**

This is one of the most valuable benefits in the entire Tax Code and why it remains my favorite section.

Please note that the following categories of property are expressly excluded from Section 1031:

- Property held primarily for sale,
- Partnership interests,
- Stocks,
- Bonds,
- Notes,
- Certificates of trust or beneficial interest, and
- Other securities or evidences of indebtedness or interest.

People sometimes ask, "Can a home builder qualify for Section 1031?" The answer is well established. No. A home builder will not qualify because their homes are held primarily for sale. The other excluded categories above would no longer qualify anyway, since the Tax Cuts & Jobs Act of 2017 excluded personal property from exchange treatment.

Section 1031 has a holding period. The relinquished property must be held for productive use in a trade or business or for investment, and the replacement property must be held in the same manner. The test is applied at the time of the exchange, without regard to the taxpayer's motives before the exchange. How long must property be held for this purpose? There is no statutory holding period, but a good rule of thumb is a minimum one-year holding period that straddles two tax returns.

Vacation homes are tricky; they may or may not qualify, depending on the amount of personal use by the taxpayer compared to the days of bona fide rentals. The determination is based on all the facts and circumstances. You should consult a qualified tax professional regarding whether a particular vacation home qualifies for exchange treatment.

Finally, foreign real property does not qualify because real property located in the United States is not "like kind" to real property located outside of the United States. What is included in the United States for this purpose? The fifty states, the District of Columbia, and the U.S. Virgin Islands. As for "like kind," we'll circle back to that concept in the next chapter.

An additional note regarding losses: Section 1031 defers gains and losses. Section 1031 is mandatory once initiated. Therefore, it is imperative not to structure an exchange when the taxpayer has a loss. In that case, you want to recognize the loss on your tax return instead of deferring it.

Chapter Two
Building Family Wealth by Exchanging

The Essentials

By exchanging over and over, taxpayers can build family wealth without taxation (federal or state). The deferred taxes are then reinvested in replacement property selected and owned by the taxpayer.

Let's make this crystal clear: you could pay the taxes and enjoy the net after-tax proceeds with no strings attached other than the loss of wealth (the tax dollars are lost forever). Or, instead of paying the taxes, you can exchange. If you exchange, the funds that would have been paid in taxes will be reinvested in replacement property. What kind of property? Another investment or business property of your choosing that you will own.

So, what is it going to be? Pay taxes or convert the tax dollars into more real estate that you will own? By exchanging in this way, family wealth is increased dramatically over time. When combined with the step up on death (when the taxes are essentially forgiven), a lifetime exchange program is one of the best methods of creating a family's financial legacy.

It is important to note that the IRS and Treasury Department have supported Section 1031 with a large body of published rulings, private rulings, and regulations to provide taxpayers with guidance on how to properly structure routine and complex exchanges, such as reverse exchanges. This makes it possible for regular folks to exchange at little cost and without risk from uncertainty. Bottom line: taxpayers need not fear an audit if they follow the rules. In addition, the courts have bent over backward to recognize exchanges. You will hear more about the famous *Starker* decision later. Even when taxpayers have made minor foot faults, courts have ruled in their favor where taxpayers intended in good faith to exchange.

Taxpayers report exchanges on IRS Form 8824 filed with the tax return for the year of the exchange. It's a complicated form, but–not to worry–most CPAs have tax software that does the heavy lifting.

Terminology

"Like-Kind Property": "Like kind" refers to the nature or character of the property and not its grade or quality. Bottom line: real property is "like kind" to other real property. This includes apartments, single-family homes, duplexes, medical offices, retail property, industrial property, commercial property, and raw land. Like kind is very broadly construed.

S ection 1031 exchanges are extremely popular and a very exciting way to build family wealth, grow your net worth, and help the economy. A lot of jobs are created around 1031 exchanges too, so when you do an exchange, you're also doing good work for America. Members of Congress and past presidents contemplated changing 1031. We are fortunate to have good data. According to a study by Ernst and Young, approximately half a million people have jobs because of Section 1031.[iii] We all pay our taxes in different ways, but as data like this demonstrates, 1031 creates a vibrant economy. As I've noted, the government still gets plenty of tax revenue, even though we're working with transactions that are tax deferred.

Because you can defer as many times as you want, we have worked with individuals who have structured seven or eight exchanges, and so they're constantly building family wealth. They are transforming what was once rental property, land held for appreciation, a farm, or property formerly used in a business. Again, we're not talking about a principal residence. Your principal residence has another Code section, Section 121, that allows you to forgive the tax, but that provision has significant limitations ($250,000 of tax forgiveness or $500,000 with your spouse).

It is important to understand that the same taxpayer that owned the relinquished property must own the replacement property. So, if you own the relinquished property in your own name, you need to own the replacement property in your own name. If it's an entity–a limited liability company, a corporation, whatever it is–use the same entity exactly. If you want to make a change, wait a year and a day, but the same entity must acquire the replacement property at closing.

An exception exists for single-member LLCs. These entities have been around for about fifteen years now, and they are referred to as "disregarded entities" or "tax nothings." They give you limited liability but do not exist for tax purposes. In conclusion, the owner of the relinquished property, whether a person or legal entity, must own the replacement property, with an exception for a single-member LLC that is owned by the original property owner.

Let's use an example. Fred owns the relinquished property in his own name (Fred is on the title). Fred must acquire the replacement property in his own name (Fred must be on the new title). However, if Fred is concerned about exposing himself to personal liability from the property, he may form a single-member LLC that is solely (100%) owned by Fred to acquire the replacement property. The single-member LLC does not exist for tax purposes; it uses Fred's taxpayer identification number and reports its activities, including the exchange, on Fred's personal income tax return. Fred will be protected from liability associated with the replacement property without adversely impacting his exchange. So, if there is liability from a slip and fall on the property, the LLC is liable and not Fred; he has protected his personal assets from liability in this manner. When you have the knowledge, it's easy to exchange without exposing all of your assets to liability. So, now you know how.

Going back to the beginning, the question at Hunton & Williams back in 1984 was the concept of "like-kind property." Section 1031 says you can exchange property for property of "like kind." What does that mean? After three days in that closet with the Lexus Nexus machine humming and generating heat at about one hundred degrees, I was able to reach the conclusion then, and it's still true today. **Any sort of real estate is "like kind" to any other sort of real estate.**

If you have a rental house and you're tired of managing the tenants, toilets, and trash, you can exchange it for virtually any sort of real estate: single-family home, apartments, shopping center, or an industrial property. It doesn't matter. The only question to ask is whether it is real estate. If it's real estate, you can exchange it for other real estate, end of story.

Some of the details can be complicated. I'll get to much of it later. What is especially interesting is that you can even exchange land, also called "unimproved real estate," for "improved real estate," where structures have been built, and vice versa. This exchange would still be considered "like kind." It's in the regulations and has been there for a long time.

"Like kind" could have been narrowly defined the way it was for personal property exchanges (before they were repealed in 2017). Do you know what is like kind to an antique Ferrari race car? Another antique Ferrari race car. Like kind in real estate could have been narrowly construed; it could have meant an apartment building for an apartment building or a single-family house for another single-family house, but the IRS and Treasury interpreted like kind exceptionally broadly–so broadly that they have encouraged exchanging. The Tax Code requires the properties to be "of like kind," and any real estate qualifies as like kind to other real estate. It's amazingly simple once you take the time to complete the research.

The like-kind standard is exceptionally broad. This flexibility allows taxpayers to exchange for more desirable types of property. For example, many real estate investors acquire rental houses in their youth. As they become older and tire of management responsibilities, they can exchange into Delaware statutory trusts (DSTs) or net-leased real estate with a passive ownership structure. Yet even passive real estate investments have many options.

At Capital Square, these various investment vehicles are our specialty, and we often help investors exchange their assets over a lifetime, while moving investment properties through various investment platforms–rental house to DSTs, DSTs to new DST replacement properties, and DSTs to a real estate investment trust (REIT) in what is known as an UPREIT transaction. Remember, those DSTs are a fractionalized real estate ownership model, meaning you might be one of numerous owners of an investment-grade property. We'll elaborate more on DSTs starting in Chapter 10. We'll discuss more about REITs, which are a different type of real estate investment vehicle involving a larger portfolio of real estate assets, in Chapter 15.

At Capital Square, we cater to different investor preferences and multi-generational wealth-building goals. Returns-oriented investors can invest solely in the development phase by investing in a development LLC. Tax-conscience real estate investors can invest in the Section 1031/DST phase. Investors with excess cash or qualified funds from an IRA, 401(k), or pension plan, who are looking to diversify risk with a steady dividend, can invest in the REIT. This value chain allows investors to remain with Capital Square, which reduces transaction costs and maximizes investor return potential, while seizing the opportunities inherent in the Tax Code.

We'll get into the intricacies of what these different types of real estate investments look like, but when it comes to 1031 exchanges, you can structure another exchange and another exchange and another exchange. You can cash out some or all if you want to, or you can continue to swap till ya' drop. We call the investors who keep swapping "serial exchangers," and that's not because they're eating Rice Krispies. That's serial with an "s," because they're exchanging over and over and over again.

You'd be surprised how many people out west do that. We have 6,500 plus exchange investors, and a large number are from California. Many are serial exchangers. They get it because their state taxes are so high it's punitive, along with the federal taxes. They've been exchanging for a long time because of rapid appreciation of real estate in their state. We have people out there on their fourth, fifth, sixth, and seventh exchanges. There are a lot of folks active like this, especially in high-tax states on the east coast (for example, New York and New Jersey), as well as out in California, where taxes are outrageously high. **Remember, Section 1031 is in the federal Tax Code, and every state conforms to Section 1031.** Pennsylvania was the last state holdout, but now even they recognize Section 1031. **So, when we talk about deferring the taxes, we are talking about deferring all the taxes–federal and state taxes.** The federal taxes come in three varieties: first, depreciation recapture, then, the capital gains tax, and, finally, the tax on net investment income for high earners (this one is a little sneaky; it comes from the Affordable Care Act).

The reason I preach the virtues of Section 1031 is to help people improve their lifestyle. Let me tell you a story. I had a wonderful client in Virginia who was a mailman. He was the nicest guy in the world. He didn't have much money, but he did have undeveloped family land. The land did not generate any income and, in fact, cost him thousands of dollars each year in taxes, insurance, and maintenance costs that he could hardly afford to pay.

A property developer came to him and said, "I want to buy your land."

And he said, "Get out of here."

When they came back again, he took out his shotgun.

He said, "Get the hell out of here. I'm not paying a million dollars in taxes, so you can build a damn Walmart on my property."

Long story short, I was sent in to talk to this mailman about Section 1031.

"Hey, don't shoot me," I said. "I just want to drink some lemonade and talk."

And he said, "Well, why are you here, boy?"

I looked him in the eye and tried to look as un-shootable as possible. "I'm here to save you a million dollars in taxes."

And he said, "Sit down."

I told him about this thing called a 1031 exchange. Once again, he told me that he wasn't going to pay a million dollars in taxes.

"I know," I said. "You are not going to pay a million dollars in taxes. You can do a Section 1031 exchange. You are not going to pay anything in taxes."

After I explained it to him, he got it. He was ready to sell, ready to sign the contract the very next day. And this mailman went from not having two nickels to rub together to having many millions of dollars of real estate. He did an exchange into income-producing real estate of his choosing, and he sent his grandkids to college. Then they went all over Europe.

He went from being a regular Joe with little money to being able to take care of his family and his grandkids. That's how 1031 took his non-income-producing land—in his case twelve undeveloped acres in the path of progress that he had been paying taxes on, as well as insurance premiums and maintenance costs—transforming from negative income to having substantial income. When his replacement properties matured, this mailman did more exchanges, and he swapped till he dropped. He didn't have to be a mailman anymore.

Regrettably, this nice man passed away a few years ago. His family inherited his real estate with a stepped-up tax basis, meaning they had the ability to sell without taxation. This is a real example of swap till ya' drop—decades of tax deferral followed by tax forgiveness.

This guy didn't have a lot of education, but he was really smart. He said later that if somebody was willing to overpay for his property, he was going to sell. He found his buyer. He found his strategy. He built dramatic family wealth through 1031 exchanges.

His story isn't a rare one. There are many reasons we exchange, but it's the opportunity to build our legacies that is exciting every single time.

Chapter Three
The Rationale
& History of 1031

The Essentials

If a taxpayer starts with real estate, ends with real estate, and never receives anything except "like-kind" property (no boot), this is a qualifying Section 1031 exchange.

Note: Any boot received will be taxable.

Terminology

"Boot": Any non-like-kind property is referred to as "boot" and is taxable. This can take the form of cash received, non-like-kind property received (for example, personal property), or reduction in debt (see discussion of debt rules in Chapter 8).

There is no problem with partial exchanges in which there is some taxable boot. However, the first dollars of taxable gain from boot generally will be taxed at 25% due to depreciation recapture.

Note: You can use bonus depreciation to offset depreciation recapture (see Chapter 9).

S ection 1031 had an especially happy birthday in 2021. That's when it turned one hundred years old. Its predecessor was first adopted in 1921, and in all these years, there have only been a few amendments, most recently eliminating personal property exchanges (for example, exchanges of trucks, rail cars, and automobiles).

While the statutory language is fairly simple, the legislative intent is unclear due to the absence of legislative history going back to 1921. As a matter of tax policy, what is the theory behind Section 1031? Professor Bradley T. Borden goes into great detail in his book on Section 1031 I've previously mentioned, describing a number of principles in support of 1031 exchanges.[iv] They include:

- Continuity of investment,
- Inequity of forcing taxpayers to pay a tax when they didn't cash out
- Administrative convenience
- Desire to increase transactions by promoting use of exchanges.

The most likely theory in support of 1031 is <u>continuity of investment.</u> You start with real estate. You end with real estate. And you never cashed out or received anything that would be taxable. You continued your investment in like-kind real estate. That means no cash, and no "non-like-kind" property. That's called "boot," and it refers to anything other than like-kind real estate included in the sale.

Back in the old days, in 1921 thinking, if you didn't receive cash, then you wouldn't have cash in your pocket to pay a tax. In other words, because you didn't receive any cash, you shouldn't have to pay a tax. It would be inequitable, unfair, to tax someone who doesn't have the cash because he or she didn't "cash out" but continued his or her investment in real estate. This was back when the tax law was fairly simplistic.

Of course, that was a long time ago. In modern times, most

exchanges are delayed with a qualified intermediary holding the exchange proceeds, pending closing on the replacement property. This means there will almost always be a break in the continuity of investment, but the theory still works at a bird's eye view because you've never had "actual" or "constructive" receipt of any cash. At the end of the process, you've continued your investment and never cashed out. You started with real estate, you ended with real estate, and you never cashed out. (Don't think about the middle of the exchange, when the qualified intermediary is holding the exchange escrow. Simply look at the end of the exchange period, when the taxpayer receives qualifying replacement property, to see the continuity of investment.)

That's how this tax-deferral model works.

That's swap till ya' drop.

Section 1031 has remained essentially the same for over one hundred years, except for a few amendments. The legislative history is unclear from this period, but in addition to Congress not wanting to impose a tax on the theoretical gain (asset appreciation), when the taxpayer continued his or her investment in like-kind property, there was likely also some recognition of the administrative inconvenience of taxing thousands of trades and exchanges each year. This was 1921. Think about all the horse trades and barters. We're swapping things. We're trading in cars and trucks and horses and buggy whips. Congress just didn't want to get involved in all that. If you do an exchange, it's just not taxable, and the real rationale may have been that it was too hard to tax all those swaps.

Finally, Professor Borden suggests that Section 1031 may have been intended to encourage property owners to enter into transactions. There is a concept called "lock in effect," where property owners do not transact due to the tax cost; they are locked in and can't reach the highest and best use for their investments. Section 1031 unlocks those property owners who can transact by structuring tax-deferred exchanges.

Have you heard of "Starker Trusts" or "Starker Exchanges"? This is another transformative moment in the history of Section 1031. If it weren't for Mr. Starker, my real estate firm, Capital Square, would not be here today. I guarantee it. This was a case that went all the way to the Ninth Circuit Court of Appeals: *Starker v. United States* (9th Cir. 1979).

Mr. Starker owned a large tract of timberland in the Northwest. But rather than selling it directly to Crown Zellerbach, a pulp and paper conglomerate on the New York Stock Exchange, Mr. Starker conveyed it without any collateral. This big company put a note on their financial statement saying that Mr. Starker had up to five years to identify replacement property of a certain value to equal the agreed value of his timberland. Crown Zellerbach would then cause the identified property to be conveyed to Mr. Starker as his replacement property.

So, Mr. Starker had up to five years to identify any number of replacement properties to match the value of his timberland. And he went out and searched. In time, he said, "Crown Zellerbach, go buy this one and convey it to me." Then he found another. "Buy this one and convey it to me." He did it again and again, and once he used up all the money on the books, the exchange was done. He had up to five years to do that, and it was held to be a good Section 1031 exchange. He never received any sales proceeds.

The courts then considered the matter of a delayed or deferred exchange. Mr. Starker conveyed his property and had up to five years to identify replacement property. You see, there was a delay between the date he conveyed his relinquished property and when he received the replacement property. There was no precedent, no authority on point. Was that allowable?

It worked its way all the way up to the Ninth Circuit Court of Appeals, ending in the Supreme Court. The case was considered, and in the end, the Ninth Circuit couldn't find any meaningful authority for or against a delayed exchange. Since they could find no valid rationale to prohibit a delayed exchange, they ruled in favor: Mr. Starker had completed a qualifying Section

1031 exchange. The court approved this delayed (or deferred) exchange, where the taxpayer conveys relinquished property on one day and acquires replacement property on a later date. The court could equally have said that this was a bad exchange, but, like many courts, the Ninth Circuit supported taxpayers who want to exchange. Delayed exchanges are the norm today, and it all goes back to Mr. Starker in the 1970s.

Before that, some people thought you had to do exchanges simultaneously. For example, I have a property, and you have a property. Then we swap our properties simultaneously, at the same time. *Starker* gave us five years to identify replacement property. But that was really too long from a tax administration standpoint. Why? Because at the outset, nobody knew what Mr. Starker had done for tax purposes. Was it an exchange? A partial exchange? A sale? An installment sale? What was it? How would Mr. Starker prepare his tax return? No one knew.

In 1984, Congress amended Section 1031 to give us forty-five days to identify replacement property and up to 180 days to close. We'll discuss these provisions in Chapters 5 and 7, but Mr. Starker, that clever guy, laid the groundwork. He was kind of like my mailman client, a thinker.

And the long exchange process wasn't the end of his clever thinking. Mr. Starker also realized that his trees grew at roughly 5% a year. He wanted interest for up to five years because his trees were growing, and the exchange was still in process. So, he said to Crown Zellerbach, "Give me a five percent growth factor, in addition to the exchange value."

The court said, "Oh, that's interesting."

The court ruled that he was taxable on the 5% just as if you had money in the bank and earned 5% interest. But it didn't blow the exchange. It was still a good exchange. He just had to pay tax on the interest. So, that's how it went. What an amazing and surprising result.

If the taxpayer is entitled to interest, logic would tell you he owns the principal, which would result in a taxable sale and not a tax-deferred exchange. This is not the only case where a court has gone out of its way to support taxpayers who, in good faith, structure exchanges, even when they are aggressive or make minor mistakes.

Crown Zellerbach bought the property, but the deal wasn't done until Mr. Starker identified and acquired the real estate assets equal to the agreed upon value. Plus, he gained that 5% growth factor. The interest was taxable but still a win because the exchange was valid.

You see, many courts have ruled favorably on 1031 exchanges. The IRS and Treasury are favorable too. The court could have said, "Well, you're entitled to the interest, but that means you own the principal." If the taxpayer owns the principal, the exchange would fail, and the transaction would be fully taxable. The court could have said, "Five years is too long." But they didn't.

Amazing case, *Starker*.

Now, things are a bit different. You can cash out a portion of the proceeds and pay tax on some, or you can reduce your debt and pay tax on the reduced debt and still do an exchange. You can do partial exchanges, and we'll come back to all that.

The Tax Cuts and Jobs Act of 2017 was also noteworthy for Section 1031 exchanges. This Act eliminated Section 1031 treatment for personal property. Fleets, trucks, and railroad cars were once exchanged by the big users. Now, they don't qualify for 1031, just real property, just real estate.

The Tax Cuts and Jobs Act also adopted several favorable new tax provisions, including a 20% pass-through deduction; bonus depreciation; and opportunity zone funds that have become very popular lately. I'll return to each of these later, but this legislation was another transformative moment for 1031.

It is important to note that an exchange will not be disqualified simply because incidental personal property is acquired along with real property, for example, furniture in an apartment building. The incidental personal property may be taxable to the extent of its value, while the remainder of the transaction (the real property) qualifies for exchange treatment.

The Tax Cuts and Jobs Act is frequently in the news. If Congress does not act, it will eventually expire. That would be a shame. Our Capital Square team members have been frequent voices in the national conversation around the advantages of making the tax benefits permanent. Signs are pointing toward this possibility. I hope so; we will see.

Chapter Four
Why Exchange?

The Essentials

The owner may exchange real property for any other real property located in the United States if the properties are held for investment or use in a business.

Terminology

"Appreciation": The increase in an asset's value

"Profit": The appreciation gained upon sale of an investment

Practice Tips

- Invest in active real estate when young, and exchange for passive real estate (for example, DSTs or net leases later in life.

- Exchange non-income-producing real estate (land) for income-producing real estate to generate cash flow.

- Acquire DSTs that have a small minimum investment to diversify and acquire higher-quality real estate.

- Change classes of real estate, tracking current market conditions for maximum profits.

W hy do we exchange? We did a little bit of this before. Let's do a bit more.

Here's what you know: Section 1031 defers the taxes from the sale of real estate. People always ask me, deferred for how long? Well, for as long as you want.

It's deferred until you sell that replacement property in a taxable transaction. But you don't have to sell it in a taxable transaction. You can always exchange it over and over again; you can swap till ya' drop, building family wealth by exchanging.

There are three major benefits of Section 1031, and we've already discussed number one in detail.

Tax deferral is the primary benefit of Section 1031.

The taxes that otherwise would be due in a taxable transaction are deferred until the replacement property is sold in a taxable transaction. The taxes may continue to be deferred over and over again in subsequent exchanges, and by deferring the taxes (federal and state), exchangers acquire more replacement property and, also, typically increase their cash flow and future profit potential. Speaking of cash flow, depreciation deductions can further increase after-tax returns by generating additional after-tax cash flow, but more on that in Chapter 9.

To sum up, instead of paying taxes on a sale, you can exchange and invest the tax dollars in replacement property of your choosing. Why pay taxes if you can instead make a plan to grow your wealth?

The second benefit comes when you can change the type of real estate that you own.

Non-income-producing real estate can be exchanged for income-producing real estate to generate income. Let's say a taxpayer owns undeveloped land. It's just sitting there. In fact, it is costing the taxpayer thousands when it comes to maintenance, repairs, insurance, and taxes. Out in the country, taxes can be low, but in bigger towns and cities, taxes can be painful–not to mention cutting the grass and keeping trespassers off the property so you won't get sued when somebody hurts themselves.

By exchanging for income-producing real estate, the taxpayer can generate an income stream, just like my mailman client. This can improve the lives of taxpayers by providing income for retirement, travel, children's education, or whatever you may want or need.

Another example of changing the type of real estate that you own is exchanging a management-intensive property, such as a rental house, for passive property, such as a DST or net lease. Think of the improvement in lifestyle if you could eliminate the hassles of real estate management and ownership.

If this is you, have you ever gotten a call in the evening that interrupted your life? Have you ever had a tenant leave food in the oven and go away, causing a kitchen fire? Yeah, they do that. I knew of one joker who put an air fryer on the deck and burned down the whole apartment building. The only good news: we had full replacement cost insurance and loss of rents coverage. So, a new building was built, and the rent continued to be paid by the insurance company.

Management-intensive property is acceptable when you're young. It's a wonderful way to build your wealth, but over time, you get busy with your career and family, and tire of active management. By exchanging management-intensive property, owners can improve their quality of life by eliminating the hassles of the three T's: tenants, toilets, and trash. Depending on who you're renting to, there's sometimes a fourth T. That's teenagers. I understand that teenagers are hellacious in the big T–Texas. It's funny the things you learn doing tax seminars across the country.

So, exchange that management-intensive property for a passive investment. It could be a net-leased property, a dollar store or pharmacy if you have enough proceeds of sale, or it could be a DST for as little as $50,000. Getting out of being a landlord can change people's lives. Frequent nights and weekends can be spent having fun or painting the house and fixing the roof.

Some feel they can't even go on vacation for fear that something's going to break.

But here's the truth: it's a great time to sell real estate. People are paying record prices for everything, everywhere. Houses are selling over asking price. Exchanging difficult properties for ones where you have no work to do but still gain the income and appreciation can be empowering. Section 1031 can indeed improve lives for exchangers beyond the benefit of tax deferral.

A third but sometimes overlooked benefit is that 1031 can be used by taxpayers to seize upon favorable real estate opportunities.

For example, if an owner of a rental or business property can sell their real estate at the top of the market and find bargains to purchase as replacement property, there's no need to turn down the offer that is too good to be true. Structuring the sale as an exchange enables beneficial transactions that can further multi-generational family wealth goals. Even our favorite mailman knew the virtues of buying low and selling high with Section 1031.

Taxpayers can improve their economic position and lifestyle by exchanging. Many CPAs will tell you that the singular benefit of Section 1031 is tax deferral for a specific period of time, and this is true. However, we have seen many taxpayers retain their replacement properties for a lifetime, converting tax deferred under Section 1031 into tax forgiveness when their heirs inherit the property.

Over the years, working with people who have sold their land, sold their rental properties, and snagged an amazing deal they might not have been able to otherwise, we've seen numerous benefits in action.

If you sell a property and pay the tax, the money's gone. But if you do an exchange, what would have been paid in taxes goes into the replacement property. You buy more property, and when that property matures, you do another exchange. You retain and compound the deferred taxes that otherwise would have been lost, and over time, you build family wealth. You create a legacy. I've seen it happen again and again, and it's amazing. That's about as good as it gets.

Chapter Five
Basic 1031 Exchange Rules & Safe Harbors

The Essentials

Section 1031 has a vesting rule: the same taxpayer that owns the relinquished property must own the replacement property. Real estate can be owned by a person or a legal entity, such as a limited liability company (LLC), limited partnership (LP), corporation, or trust. There is one exception for single-member LLCs, because a single-member LLC is a disregarded entity, meaning that it does not exist for tax purposes. It is a tax nothing. You can form a single-member LLC that is owned 100% by the taxpayer, no problem. This is done mostly for liability protection. If the relinquished property is owned by a natural person, a single-member LLC owned by that person provides liability protection and does not adversely impact the exchange.

Terminology

"Vesting": Vesting relates to the process of becoming an owner; it is the moment in time when legal ownership of a property is officially transferred from a seller to a buyer.

"Qualified Intermediary": Sometimes referred to as an "exchange accommodator," a qualified intermediary (QI) facilitates Section 1031 exchanges. To qualify for 1031 exchange treatment, taxpayers must avoid actual or constructive receipt of the proceeds of sale from the relinquished property. This is not an issue for taxpayers who use a QI because the regulations provide a "safe harbor" when following the rules.

"Safe Harbor": The IRS and Treasury provide a "safe harbor" for qualified intermediaries. By following the safe harbor, exchangers need not worry about making certain technical errors that would disqualify their exchanges.

T he one thing that will kill an exchange every time–100% of the time–is taking possession of the cash. This is what we call "actual receipt," whether the taxpayer goes to closing and the money is wired into their account or if the taxpayer deposits a check. Whatever it is, when the cash is received, that's a done deal. It's the same if the sale proceeds go to the taxpayer's agent, their lawyer, their CPA, financial advisor, or their second cousin before delivering it to the taxpayer. Those situations would be "constructive receipt," meaning that the funds are received by the taxpayer "constructively" as the lawyers say–in other words, via an agent.

You can't have actual receipt and still move forward with a 1031 exchange. You can't have constructive receipt either, where the cash moves through an agent.

The IRS and Treasury created "safe harbors" in the regulations. If you follow one of the safe harbors, the money–meaning the net proceeds of sale from your relinquished property–will be held by the QI, and under the safe harbor, the proceeds of sale will not be deemed your money.

You could think of this as a fiction since the proceeds ultimately belong to the taxpayer. The IRS and Treasury established a way for anyone to exchange, even an unsophisticated person. The safe harbors are authorized and approved. Use them to avoid technical defaults.

Specifically, four safe harbors are provided in the regulations that protect the taxpayer from being taxable as a result of actual or constructive receipt of the exchange funds. These are:

1. Use of a Qualified Intermediary to facilitate the exchange–the most common
2. Use of a Qualified Escrow or Trust to hold the exchange proceeds–very rarely used
3. Use of a Guarantee or Security Arrangement to secure the exchange proceeds–very rarely used

4. Interest paid on exchange proceeds–common in most exchanges

Typically, some amount of interest is paid on the exchange escrow. This safe harbor is applicable when interest is earned on the exchange escrow account, ratifying the second holding in the *Starker* case. In addition, Revenue Procedure 2000-37 provides a safe harbor for reverse exchanges, but that's a different story.

Most exchanges today are structured using the qualified intermediary safe harbor, and this is what we use most of the time at Capital Square. A qualified intermediary (QI) can be an affiliate of the title company or escrow company. The bank could be a QI, offering qualified intermediary services, or the QI could be any number of people or firms that specialize in providing exchange services. They are often affiliated with a party who would be at the closing anyway. They are experienced and accustomed to facilitating exchanges.

What is the QI's role? The QI facilitates the exchange by preparing the Exchange Agreement that should be signed by the taxpayer and the QI prior to closing on the relinquished property. Then, when the relinquished property is sold, the QI holds the net proceeds of sale in a manner that satisfies the safe harbor.

The Exchange Agreement is a special document that complies with the terms of the safe harbor. So, the money sits outside of the taxpayer's hands, in a bank or investment account, waiting for the taxpayer to identify replacement property. The key is, it's a safe harbor. You don't have to worry about inadvertently triggering the taxes if you follow the rules of the safe harbor.

There are many different kinds of exchanges, but the ones we talk about the most are delayed exchanges. A delayed exchange operates as follows: prior to closing on the sale of your relinquished property, you sign an Exchange Agreement that satisfies the safe harbor and directs the closing agent to deliver your net proceeds to the QI. Then, you convey your relinquished property to the buyer, and here we go, the net proceeds are delivered to the QI to be used for your replacement property (or returned to you if not used). You were the seller and become an exchanger.

At this point, you become a buyer. You've sold your property. You're doing an exchange. You need to find another property, a replacement property.

Then, within the proper timing–not five years like Starker but within a tighter but workable timetable–you find a replacement property (or properties) you like. You put it under contract. When the time comes to close, you direct the QI to pay the seller of the replacement property. At closing, the seller conveys the replacement property directly to the exchanger/buyer, and everything's done. It's simple. It works like magic and all that for a QI fee of about $1,000 for a basic exchange.

Note: all deeds are direct (exchanger/seller to buyer and seller to exchanger/buyer). The QI is never in the chain of title. There are no unnecessary deeds or transfer costs.

The exchange proceeds sit in the qualified intermediary's exchange escrow account until you find the right like-kind real estate–meaning any type of real estate–and then you're ready to go. If you don't do anything, you just get your money back, and you pay your taxes. Again, it works simply and really well.

Back in the dark days, we didn't have a road map on how to structure an exchange. For example, the most basic question was, "Who is going to hold the proceeds of sale from the relinquished property pending purchase of the replacement property?"

The seller/taxpayer couldn't hold the funds. That would be actual receipt and taxable every time. The logical party was the taxpayer's attorney, but that might constitute constructive receipt; the same is true for other agents, such as accountants, financial advisors, and the like. If the buyer is to hold the funds, what if the buyer has "buyer's remorse" and won't disburse the funds when needed to purchase the replace-

ment property? Do you actually need the buyer's coopera-
tion? If so, the buyer may want something for cooperating.
How about using a bank to hold the exchange escrow?
That might be possible, but banks are reluctant to get in the
middle of a transaction, especially one with tax ramifications
where the rules are unclear. But with the safe harbor, we don't
need the buyer, agents, or others to cooperate. We simply
need to hire a QI, sign a standard Exchange Agreement, and
follow the rules.

As mentioned, roughly 20–25% of all commercial real
estate transactions are likely structured as exchanges.
That's a lot. That's why Congress hasn't modified Section 1031
for real estate. Doing so would crash the real estate market.
There are so many exchanges going on now.

As you know, Mr. Starker had five years for this process.
Just think about that. It must have been an administrative
nightmare to report the transaction on his tax return. Is it a
taxable sale? Is it an exchange? Is it an installment sale? At the
outset, there's no way of knowing.

Thus, Congress said, and I'm paraphrasing, "We're going
to create rules that will give you some time. But you can't
take five years. That's ridiculous. Instead, when you've sold
a relinquished property, you have forty-five days to acquire
all of your replacement property. If you are not ready by the
forty-fifth day, you can 'identify' replacement property by
midnight of the forty-fifth day, which will give you up to
180 days from the original closing date to acquire all of your
replacement property."

Exchangers can use that additional time to finish their
due diligence, obtain financing, and do all the things they
need to do. The same is true whether exchanging for one or
more replacement properties.

**Note: Time starts for both the forty-five-day identifi-
cation and 180-day closing period when the relinquished
property is transferred for tax purposes. This occurs when**

the benefits and burdens of ownership transfer from seller to buyer. That date is not always determined by the settlement statement. For example, let's say the settlement statement has the date of Friday, but the courthouse is closed because Friday is a bank holiday. The benefits and burdens of ownership may not pass from seller to buyer until Monday or even Tuesday, when the deed is recorded and the buyer becomes the owner for tax purposes. A helpful tip: if you happen to be short on days for purposes of the forty-five-day identification or 180-day closing periods, you should confirm the actual date of closing, because the date on the settlement statement may not be the actual day for tax purposes. If so, you may have more time to identify and close on the replacement property.

Continuing the conversation, to qualify for the safe harbor, the Exchange Agreement must limit the exchanger's rights to receive, pledge, borrow, or otherwise receive the benefit of the exchange proceeds*, except:

1. After the end of the forty-five-day identification period, if the exchanger has not identified any replacement property; or
2. If the exchanger has identified replacement property, then upon or after receipt by exchanger of all replacement property to which exchanger is entitled under the Exchange Agreement; or
3. If the exchanger has identified replacement property, then upon or after the occurrence, after the end of the identification period, of a material and substantial contingency that:
    *   relates to the exchange,
    *   is provided for in writing, and
    *   is beyond the control of exchanger and of any disqualified party, other than the party obligated to transfer replacement property to exchanger; or
4. After the end of the 180-day exchange period.

* The so-called "(g)(6)" restrictions, which are critical in a properly drafted Exchange Agreement

These are the conditions that permit cashing out of the exchange escrow. In many cases, it will be 181 days before the taxpayer can cash out. The taxpayer may cash out sooner if no properties are identified or if all the identified properties have been acquired.

Yes, this all sounds very complicated, but once we get into things, you can see that it's really not so complex. At Capital Square, we can help alleviate a lot of stress by having a portfolio of qualifying DST replacement properties that can be identified and acquired quickly and easily.

We find that people show up, interested in doing an exchange, and they say, "I'm not sure what I want."

That's where Capital Square comes in. Working with the exchanger's advisors, we ask, "Do you want to invest in a new Class A multifamily community, an older Class B multifamily community with value add, a build-for-rent community, a medical office, or an industrial property?"

If they still look at us with a blank expression on their faces, we simplify our questions even more.

"What are your goals for this investment? Are you familiar with the pros and cons of different types of assets and different types of real estate investment vehicles?"

Sometimes, we spend a lot of time talking through various opportunities. And typically, within a matter of days, after some comprehensive education about the different types of available real estate offerings, they can narrow it down, and it's usually quick. Our business is based on numerous DST offerings being available at any given time, ready to suit the needs of different exchangers. Because, as you know, investors have different desires and needs. Many investors have their own advisors; we work seamlessly with advisors and become part of the exchange team to make for an efficient process.

Now, if you're a house flipper, trying to buy a new rental house, you might get out there, and after the first twenty days or so, there is nothing you're excited about. Or maybe a couple appeared. Maybe you want to identify them as your replacement property, giving you 180 days to close on them. It can be a stressful process. The clock keeps ticking. If they're not under contract and through your due diligence process, you could lose out.

We encourage people to close within forty-five days to avoid the identification process entirely. And our process is efficient and makes it easy to close within those forty-five days.

Not everyone's is. We once had a call from a friend of a friend, whose colleague had $95 million sitting with the QI, with twenty days left to identify their replacement property because their first property didn't pass due diligence. It had a devastating environmental issue. It was a wipeout. Now, they had twenty days left to find $95 million of replacement property, and they were getting extremely nervous.

There aren't that many $95 million properties out there, ready to go; fortunately for the taxpayer, Capital Square had a large inventory of qualifying Delaware statutory trust replacement properties. We'll get to our DST offerings shortly, where we've already done the work: we bought the properties; all the due diligence is done; the loans are in place; and they can be closed in a matter of days. But we'll dig into those weeds in Chapter 10.

In short, be careful with identifying your replacement property. The identification simply means it is on a list of properties that may be acquired in the exchange; this is for tax purposes. It doesn't mean that you can actually buy the property or that you will want to own the property. The best practice is to have replacement property under binding contract, to have completed all of your due diligence, and to have any required debt committed from a lender before the expiration of the forty five-day identification period. I've known people who have identified properties, and all of them flamed out—they had no options. So, if you're preparing your ID list of replacement properties, make sure you can close on one (or more) of them in an amount that will fully satisfy your equity and debt requirements under Section 1031. You have up to 180 days after the relinquished property closing to acquire replacement property, but after forty-five days, you can only acquire properties on the ID list. And if you close on all replacement properties within forty-five days, there is no need to identify at all; that is my strong preference.

If you identify, the ID must be in writing and delivered to your QI. In your Exchange Agreement package, there's usually an identification form that you should complete. Nowadays, you'll scan it and send it digitally, shooting a picture of it to your QI, and they'll acknowledge receipt. Twenty or so years ago, we used fax machines. We did hundreds of exchanges, and then we went back to audit the ID letters. Remember when fax machine paper faded to white? They were all gone, and there was nothing anybody could do about it. Everyone of them, hundreds of exchanges, had no record, no proof of identification. Luckily, we had original ID letters in another file.

Did I tell you that for a time I was a QI? That is until I woke up one day and realized that I was holding hundreds of millions of dollars and that was too much for such a modest fee.

As an additional note, remember the value of identifying multiple replacement properties during this process. The whole point for some exchangers is to buy more time to find replacement properties; house flippers want more time to play the market. If you always identify three properties of any value (the three-property identification rule)– or more than three if that suits you–as long as the total fair market value doesn't exceed 200% of what you sold (the 200% identification rule), it's okay. So, for example, if you sold a $100,000 property, you could identify three properties that total $500,000 or even $1,000,000 (no limit on their value). If you use the three-property rule and close on one or more of them, it's a good exchange. The necessary requirements were met, even if some of the identified properties didn't end up coming into play. The same is true with the 200% rule as long as you do not exceed 200% in the value of your identified properties. Note: we will walk through these specifics in more detail, with one investor's experience, in Chapter 7.

Having a trusted partner at your side as you navigate Section 1031 can make all the difference. It can be straightforward, and it feels that way to us. We live, breathe, and sleep this stuff. We love it.

A few decades ago, I was in Washington for a conference on a private ruling request about a novel 1031 issue dealing with tenant in common ownership. You can ask for a conference with the IRS/Treasury officials responsible for a ruling, so that's what we were there doing. We were making the case for why our transaction should qualify under Section 1031.

After a while, we needed a break, and a nice lady who worked at Treasury said something along the lines of, "You know, my mom has a rental house, and it's driving her crazy. The roof leaks, and the tenant doesn't pay the rent. It's worth a lot of money, but she has no tax basis in it. She can't afford to sell because of the taxes. There are no rules on how to structure a Section 1031 exchange, and she can't afford a fancy tax lawyer like you to structure an exchange on her rental house. Why can't my mom do an exchange?"

She looked at me and kept going before we could answer.

"Your wealthy clients can afford to do exchanges. Big companies can afford to have tax lawyers. My mom can't do this because it would cost too much to do an exchange on her little rental house."

The funny thing is, just before the next Thanksgiving holiday, regulations were issued creating safe harbors for qualified intermediaries that allow anybody to do an exchange for a very small cost. Personally, I have a feeling that after our conference, that nice lady went back and said, "We need to create some rules so regular folks like my mom can do an exchange." And guess who spent all of the Thanksgiving holiday that year learning the new regulations, including the safe harbor for qualified intermediaries?

She's probably retired by now. I wonder about her mother's legacy built from a heartfelt request to provide simple rules so that regular folks can enjoy the benefits of exchanging. Section 1031 has evolved over the years, but it's only gotten better during my roughly forty-year courtship with the Code. Hopefully, that lady's family had the opportunity to take advantage of it. Hopefully, the more you learn, the more you can discover your profound possibilities too.

Chapter Six
Exchange Myths

The Essentials

When it comes to myths about Section 1031 exchanges, most can be busted by understanding three basic ideas:

1. Section 1031 defers taxes, and that deferral may become permanent on death.

2. Investment or business real estate qualifies. Investment real estate may be held for income production, appreciation, or a combination of the two.

3. Principal residences and second homes do not qualify. Real estate outside the United States does not qualify.

Specific Tax Codes

§ 1031: Defers taxes; does not forgive them (but there is a step up in basis on death)

§ 1033: Involuntary conversions (casualty/condemnation)

§ 121: Tax is forgiven on the sale of principal residence (limited to $250,000/$500,000 with spouse)

§ 1400Z-1: Tax is forgiven in a qualified opportunity zone fund if the investment is held for ten years and certain requirements are satisfied.

The general rule in the Tax Code is gain recognition. Typically, gain is recognized, meaning it is taxable. You sell property, and you pay taxes on the gain. Section 1031 is an exception to that rule. It's an exception that's been around for over one hundred years. People sometimes say that this is underhanded: "You're cheating. This is bad stuff."

It's not. It's in the Code. It's an established exception to the general rule of gain recognition.

Section 1031 has been there since 1921, over one hundred years. Congress supports the provision, along with the IRS and Treasury Department, who have provided a large body of regulations and rulings, including "safe harbors" to make it possible for regular folks to exchange. In addition, the courts have bent over backward to recognize exchanges, such as the Starker decision, where taxpayers aim to exchange in good faith. Even when taxpayers have made minor foot faults, courts have ruled in their favor when the taxpayers intended to exchange. So, Section 1031 has been examined. It's been tested. It's good stuff. Not to worry.

So many myths linger when it comes to financial strategies, so let's spend some time on seven falsehoods that I hear from concerned exchangers. You must be thoughtful as you seek to grow your wealth. Having the correct information is the differentiator.

I'm so close to it, doing exchanges since 1984, when that spring I had one of the happiest days of my life, because Hunton & Williams called and said, "You're going to be our newest tax lawyer."

"Great," I said. "I'm on my way, literally and figuratively."

The firm called, and, the next day, I arrived in my dad's old Ford Granada, wearing a new suit. I didn't know much then. But I do now.

Here are the top seven myths I hear about Section 1031 exchanges:

1. Exchangers have to find someone with property who will swap property for property with them.
2. Exchangers have to buy the same type of real estate that they are exchanging.
3. Exchangers have to complete the exchange in one simultaneous transaction.
4. Exchanges are expensive, difficult, and only for the wealthy.
5. Section 1031 is a red flag for an IRS audit.
6. An exchanger who lives on part of his or her property cannot exchange.
7. Exchangers do not need to hire a qualified intermediary (QI). They can simply have their brother-in-law, CPA, or personal attorney hold the exchange funds until the replacement property is purchased.

There are a lot of falsehoods people have in their minds about exchanging. Let's go through them one by one.

First, some think you must swap with somebody who has a property that you want in exchange. You have a property, and I have a property. Then we meet in the middle and swap. But it doesn't work like that anymore. Maybe in 1920s America, but no longer. You don't need any special help with your exchange from the buyer of your relinquished property or the seller of your replacement property. You don't need to find somebody to swap with you. That's a misnomer from the old days. Please stop worrying about this unnecessary complication.

Some people think they have to acquire the same type of real estate that they're exchanging, but you don't. I've said it before, but it's worth repeating. You don't have to buy another duplex when you sell your old duplex; nor do you have to buy more undeveloped land when selling the acres that have been in your family for generations. You could sell that rental property and exchange for a DST that is a fractional ownership in a multifamily apartment community. You could exchange those undeveloped acres for a build-for-rent (BFR) single-family housing community. Your only restraint is that the replacement property must be "like kind," and as we've discussed, that means it has to be any other type of real estate in the United States that is to be held for investment or use in a business. Again, this is not real estate for personal use, and we're not talking about your principal residence, a second home, or real estate abroad.

Some people think that the exchange has to happen all at once, a simultaneous exchange. Out of the thousands of exchanges I have worked on throughout my career, I can only remember one or two simultaneous exchanges. And these were big efforts because they are so rare. Almost all Section 1031 exchanges these days are delayed or deferred exchanges. Somebody wants to buy your property, and you structure the sale as an exchange for tax purposes. Then, as a next step, you go and become a buyer of the replacement property, and you buy from somebody else. That new property becomes your replacement property in the exchange: taxpayer/seller to buyer and, later, seller to taxpayer/buyer. We are talking about three parties with the QI as the fourth party in the middle receiving the net proceeds of the relinquished property sale and funding the purchase price for the replacement property purchase. Remember the Starker exchange? We don't have five years anymore, but Mr. Starker and the Ninth Circuit Court of Appeals are your reminders that simultaneous exchanges aren't necessary.

People think Section 1031 exchanges are difficult, expensive, and only for rich people. That's a myth; it's simply not so. The qualified intermediaries (QIs) do a great job of being cost effective. Simple exchanges can be completed for a QI fee of approximately $1,000, plus a few bucks for additional replacement properties. Remember the mailman who didn't have two nickels to rub together? He saw the value in the opportunity and made it happen. Exchanges have become simple additions to a routine real estate closing; they are accessible to anyone.

Some people fear being audited, but we've had almost no audits in forty years of exchanging. I can only think of two. One when there was a math error on Form 8824. This is a predictable result: if the form does not add up, you may be audited. In the other case, the taxpayers were finagling things, if you know what I mean. They were not following the rules, and they should have been audited. But that's two out of many thousands. In fact, in fiscal year 2023, only 0.2% of individual income tax returns filed for 2021 were audited. The same number was true for the year prior.[v]

Exchanges are not a red flag for an audit. That's another myth. Follow the law. Follow Section 1031. Hire a QI. Complete Form 8824 accurately. Nowadays, it's computer generated. You plug in the numbers, and it automatically computes the math correctly. Completing tax returns is a breeze for the CPAs of the world. I'm going to leave it to them. That is not much fun for me; I'm happy they love it. My only advice is not to check the "related party exchange" box on Form 8824. (See Appendix C.) If you're going to do a related party exchange, you better hire an experienced tax professional and make sure you get it right.

Now if you're familiar with my company, you might know that Capital Square has an independent audit conducted on all DST properties annually. We are a real estate company with a focus on tax-advantaged real estate investments. Thus, we do our due diligence, and as a principled and responsible firm, all of our DST programs are audited annually by an independent CPA firm. Also, Capital Square's financials have been audited annually since formation. Property and firm audits for transparency and accountability are the best practice, while IRS audits of exchanges are not a serious concern.

Still, after all this, the myths continue. One more that I can use my own story to disprove is the notion that if you live on part of a property, you cannot do an exchange. But you can. It's a matter of dividing the property–separating the sale of your principal residence for tax exclusion under Section 121 from the balance of the property for an exchange. I've set up my own farm and principal residence this way to make it easier. I might not have mentioned yet that I'm an amateur equestrian. I love horses. We own an equestrian facility that is leased to Joan, who operates the farm as a business; we receive a monthly income, and the tenant runs the farm. The farm is owned by a limited liability company that is owned by Paula, my wife, and me. Paula and I personally own the adjoining principal residence. When the time comes to move on to assisted living, we will be able to exchange the farm (investment property) and sell the residence (principal residence, owned with a spouse, meaning $500,000 of tax forgiveness).

Speaking of the tricky stuff, qualified intermediaries sound like they're pretty tricky. They aren't. They simply prepare the necessary Exchange Agreement and hold the exchange proceeds in compliance with the IRS safe harbor described in Chapter 5. **Taxpayers should always use a QI to obtain the safe harbor for a successful 1031 exchange.**

In short, there are a lot of myths out there, but I will say this: there are two scenarios where taxpayers lose every time. First, failure to sign an Exchange Agreement before closing on the relinquished property is death to an exchange, and there is no cure. Note: you have up to the instant of closing the relinquished property to sign an Exchange Agreement; last-minute exchanges are still good exchanges. Second, is a similar scenario, when a taxpayer takes possession of the proceeds of sale. Let's say you go to closing, selling your real estate, and you take possession of the cash. Then one minute later, you say, "Oh my gosh, I want to do an exchange." It's too late. Actual receipt results in complete taxation. The same is true if the proceeds of sale are received by your agent (for example, your attorney, CPA, financial advisor, etc.). Your only other option at this point is to invest in a qualified opportunity zone fund to defer and exclude the taxable gain. Luckily, I also discuss those for you in Chapter 14.

It's best to have a plan before closing. You call the qualified intermediary, who we'll discuss more in a moment; you sign an Exchange Agreement; and you're okay to make this choice right up until the instant when ownership transfers for tax purposes. After ownership transfers, there's no flexibility—you are 100% taxable.

Back in the day, I would routinely get calls from the law firm around 4:00 p.m. on a Friday, telling me a seller wants to convert their sale into an exchange.

"No problem," I'd say. "Our trustworthy legal assistant, Julia, can prepare the necessary Exchange Agreement in about fifteen minutes and deliver it to closing, just in time."

So, if a sale is converted to an exchange the instant before closing, that's fine too.

I repeat: no problem. But not one second after closing.

Chapter Seven
Deferred/Delayed Exchanges in Action

The Essentials

There are many types of exchanges, including:

1. Delayed or deferred
2. Simultaneous
3. Build-to-Suit
4. Reverse
5. Reverse Build-to-Suit

Our discussions focus on delayed or deferred exchanges, which are the most common. Simultaneous exchanges are rare. Related-party exchanges are typically much more complex and fairly rare; they are to be avoided if possible. The IRS has been concerned about a concept called "basis shifting" that may create an unfair tax advantage for taxpayers. To limit this conduct, Congress adopted Section 1031(f), to disqualify certain transactions among related parties who do not hold their properties received in the exchange for two years. This is a complex topic that should be approached with guidance from a qualified tax professional or, better still, avoided.

As noted, there is information for related-party exchanges on Form 8824 (see Appendix C), which suggests this may be an audit risk that should be avoided.

Practice Tip

Always engage a qualified intermediary (QI) and sign the Exchange Agreement before closing the relinquished property. The taxpayer has up to the moment of closing to insert the QI by signing an Exchange Agreement. Then, the proceeds of sale will be held by the QI in an exchange escrow account to be used to acquire replacement property or, alternatively, will be returned to the taxpayer to the extent not used in the exchange. The QI will fund earnest money deposits and the purchase price for the replacement property out of the exchange escrow account upon written direction from the taxpayer.

While the funds in the exchange escrow account ultimately belong to the taxpayer, for up to 180 days, the funds will be held by the QI. At the end of the 180-day closing period, the funds will be disbursed to the exchanger to the extent not used to acquire replacement property. In rare circumstances, it may be possible to cash out earlier. (See my discussions of cashing out in Chapters 5 and 9.)

We've talked about Mr. Starker, who owned timberland in the West. Mr. Starker made a deal with a large public company to convey his property to the buyer for a stated purchase price and had up to five years to identify replacement property in the amount of the purchase price, in what we call a "delayed" or "deferred" exchange. Before the *Starker* decision, it was unclear if a delayed exchange would qualify under Section 1031.

Starker v. United States (9th Cir. 1979) was the seminal case that laid the groundwork for today's exchange industry. This decision held that Mr. Starker's transaction qualified for Section 1031 exchange treatment, approving a delayed exchange. However, the powers that be also knew that five years was a long time. How would Mr. Starker report the transaction for tax purposes? Was it an exchange, an installment sale, a taxable sale, a partial exchange? Who knows? At the outset, there was no way to tell.

Soon thereafter, in 1984, Congress deemed five years too long and imposed the **forty-five-day identification** and **180-day closing rules.** If the taxpayer closes on all replacement properties within forty-five days, there is no need to identify. If the taxpayer has not closed on all replacement properties by midnight of the forty-fifth day, the taxpayer may buy more time by identifying replacement property, which is done by sending the QI a list of potential replacement properties. In other words, taxpayers have forty-five days to play the market; if they want longer, they must follow the strict rules governing identification and closing of replacement property. And 180 days is the maximum to close on all replacement properties, barring a Presidentially declared emergency.

Regarding delayed exchange requirements, if the taxpayer has not closed on all replacement properties within forty-five days, the following rules will apply:

1. **Forty-Five-Day Identification Rule:** The exchanger must identify potential replacement property (or properties) within forty-five days of closing the reliquished property.

2. **180-Day Closing Rule:** The exchanger must acquire all replacement property within 180 days of closing the relinquished property or the due date of the exchanger's tax return (including extensions) for the year of transfer of the relinquished property (whichever occurs first). Since most taxpayers can file extensions, taxpayers usually have the full 180 days.

3. **There are no extensions for any reason** (other than a Presidentially declared emergency).

4. **Time begins to run on the day the exchanger transfers the relinquished property to the buyer.** This is the date that the benefits and burdens of ownership pass to the buyer for tax purposes (not necessarily the date shown on the settlement statement).

5. **The time limits are strictly construed.**

For this purpose, these days are calendar days, including weekends and holidays. It is irrelevant if a deadline falls on a holiday or weekend–the date is the deadline. If the forty-fifth day is Christmas, New Year's, or your mother's birthday, there are no excuses. There is only one exception: a Presidentially declared emergency that extends tax due dates.

For Mr. Starker, who had up to five years to acquire replacement property, there was no limitation on the number of replacement properties he could identify. He could have identified every property in the New York City phone book, a massive number of properties. It was not surprising that the IRS and Treasury deemed that to be excessive and, in 1991, imposed limitations on the identification of multiple properties.

Regarding property identification requirements, if the taxpayer has not closed on all replacement properties within forty-five days, the following rules will apply:

1. **Three Property Rule:** The exchanger may identify up to three properties of any value.
2. **200% Rule:** The exchanger may identify more than three properties if the gross unencumbered fair market value of all identified properties does not exceed 200% of the gross unencumbered fair market value of the relinquished property.
3. **95% Exception:** If the exchanger identifies properties in excess of rules one and two, then the exchanger must acquire 95% of the value of all properties identified.

Note: The rules described above will not apply when the taxpayer has acquired all replacement properties within forty-five days. That means there are no limits on the number of replacement properties that can be acquired, provided all are closed within forty-five days. If the taxpayer needs more time, then the rules above will apply. Finally, once the taxpayer has acquired all identified replacement properties, the exchange is complete.

Strict compliance with the rules is required. If the exchanger violates the rules, even in a minor way, the exchange is fully taxable. For example, if he or she identifies four properties or 201% in value, the exchange is 100% taxable. Failure to properly identify replacement property by midnight of the forty-fifth day results in the total failure of the exchange. Even a minor violation will result in total failure of the proposed exchange.

Note: The IRS and courts have been very generous in other areas but, be warned, the identification and closing rules are strictly construed—foot faults are deadly; you must avoid them.

The identification rules are highly technical. Exchangers should seek the advice of a qualified tax professional for any questions. The three-property rule, for example, seems very straightforward, but what is a "property"? Is the shopping center and its parking lot across the street (not contiguous) one property or two? A careful reading of the literature is required to reach the correct conclusion.

Now, you say that you want to identify a whole lot of properties. That's great. If you want to identify more than three properties, then there's the 200% rule. You can identify an unlimited number of properties up to 200% of the gross unencumbered, fair market value of your relinquished property. That's a lot of words, and oftentimes replacement property is not on the market. So, how can you tell what it's worth? Here's where you need to be careful. Only use the 200% rule with help from experienced tax professionals. Remember, the qualified intermediary doesn't technically give tax advice. They'll guide you on the basics, but you cannot rely on the QI because they are not intended to give tax advice. That's not their business. Work with a professional–a tax lawyer, a CPA, a financial advisor if a DST, or someone thoroughly familiar with these rules–and don't put yourself in a bad spot.

And then there's a 95% exception if you over-iden-tify, but then you acquire 95% by value. Lord knows why this rule is here. To help a taxpayer who over-iden-tifies? Who says the IRS doesn't have a heart? The regulation continues that if you acquire 95% of the identified properties by value, then you're okay, even if you over-identified. But be careful. Bottom line: following the strict technicalities leads to a successful exchange.

Procedures for Identification:

1. The identification must be delivered to the intermediary.
2. The identification must be in writing and signed by the exchanger.
3. The identification must be "unambiguous" (site specific).
4. The identification must be delivered, mailed, faxed, or "otherwise sent" within forty-five days of the sale of the relinquished property.

An identification sent early may be revoked within forty-five days, and a new identification can be substituted in its place.

Talking through the legal requirements is one thing, but seeing all of this in action can aid understanding. Bad logistics can create wipeouts. Good logistics create smooth exchanges.

Imagine a retired administrator and widow who has owned an investment property for a long time (very low tax basis). Let's call her Sally. She relies on the rental income to supplement her modest pension. The property has appreciated dramatically over the years and is encumbered by a small mortgage ($250,000). She lives in a state that imposes a very high capital gains tax, not to mention federal recapture and capital gains taxes.

Sally received an unsolicited offer to buy the property for $1 million, a price that was too good to turn down. She did not have a realtor but signed the contract with no contingencies and a short closing date. As a widow with modest resources, she is very concerned about the impact of taxes. Will she have sufficient income for her golden years? Can she provide a legacy for her children and grandchildren when she dies?

Luckily, Sally has heard about Section 1031. Before closing, she engages a QI and signs an Exchange Agreement. At closing, the net proceeds of sale less the loan pay-off are wired directly to the QI in accordance with the Exchange Agreement. The date of closing is day zero, and the 45/180-day clock has started to tick. Funny story: some people think the day of closing is day one. Remember Y2K? Dates can be confusing. But the day of closing starts the 1031 clock; the next day is day one.

Sally is not a real estate professional. She does not have a lawyer, CPA, or financial advisor to help her. Sally sold her relinquished property for $1 million less the $250,000 loan payoff and $25,000 of closing costs. Thus, she has $725,000 in the exchange escrow and must have debt of $250,000 (or greater) on the replacement property to complete an exchange. That means she needs to acquire a replacement property that costs at least $975,000, including closing costs. Note: she can always trade up to a more costly replacement property using debt or cash from another source.

Her journey might play out like this:

Day one through seven:
The first week, she talks to realtors to find replacement property but has not found the right person to help her find replacement property. Toward the end of the week, she finds a realtor that she really likes.

Day eight through nineteen:
Sally and her realtor explore replacement property options, but nothing is quite right.

Day twenty through thirty:
By day twenty, she doesn't have a replacement property, and Sally is feeling a bit of time pressure. The realtor continues to present many options. Rental houses and net leases appear to be the best candidates, so she begins the process of narrowing down the list to find the right property. Sally decides to identify three rental houses in her town that are listed for sale from $975,000 to $1 million, a purchase price that works for the exchange.

Day thirty through forty:
By day thirty, Sally wants to inspect the properties and conduct due diligence, for example, reviewing the leases and confirming that the houses comply with applicable laws. Because she doesn't have an attorney who can help on the legal front or a CPA who can help her assess the tax consequences, she struggles but eventually finds a qualified attorney and CPA. This takes her to day forty.

Day forty through forty-five:
Now, with her back against the wall, she decides to make a three-property identification. She is able to inspect two of the rental houses in her town but not the third.

Day forty-five, Identification Day:

On day forty-five, with the realtor's help, Sally identifies three rental houses; she declines to identify a net-leased dollar store located out of state. She completes the form of identification letter that is attached to her Exchange Agreement and emails the form to the QI with a cc to her lawyer and realtor. The QI confirms receipt in writing before midnight of the forty-fifth day, completing the identification requirement.

With the pressure somewhat off, she begins considering her replacement property. The 180-day closing deadline does not seem onerous, but she is diligent and wants to get the cash flowing again from her replacement property. What happens next surprises her.

Sally prefers rental houses but did not have them under contract. The first and second houses are sold to a house flipper before she and her realtor submit an offer. She is able to put the third house under contract, but during the due diligence period, her attorney discovers that the seller does not have good title. This is the third house that she hadn't had time to inspect. The process to clear title could take a very long time, well beyond the 180-day closing requirement, meaning that her exchange is a total wipe out–100% taxable. This happens all too often. **The technicalities of exchange identification are one thing, but don't forget you actually need to purchase the property.**

This could have been avoided by assembling a team of professionals at an earlier date to better plan for a whole property or DST replacement property. By the way, many DST properties are available at all times with debt in place plus an easy identification and closing process, as we will discuss in later chapters. If only she had identified a DST as her third property, she would have a fallback and could have closed her exchange in a matter of days. Don't make this mistake on your exchanges.

Let's examine an alternative scenario. Let's say Sally is able to purchase one of the houses, but the successful purchase of replacement property doesn't always mean that all is well.

Now, it comes as a surprise to Sally that she must have equal or greater debt on the replacement property for a complete exchange. She has not applied for a mortgage in many decades and does not know where to go. She is referred to several mortgage brokers but discovers that the community banks in her town who usually lend on rental houses are not interested. They don't find her to be a great borrower because she is retired.

If unable to obtain a loan, she will be taxable on the $250,000 of debt. And the tax will be at the highest federal rate of 25% on depreciation previously claimed with the balance at the capital gains rate plus state tax. Worse than that, without a loan, she does not have enough proceeds to purchase the house. Her proposed exchange is a total failure, and the entire tax will be due; she will have lost a wonderful source of supplemental income in her golden years. Ouch!

Sally would have had a better shot if, from the start, she had a realtor and financial advisor familiar with Section 1031 exchanges. With the right professional partners, she could have charted a much easier path to complete tax deferral, building wealth for herself and for future generations.

The moral of Sally's story: assemble a team of experienced professionals at an early date, including a real estate attorney, CPA, specialized financial advisor (if pursuing a DST), realtor, and a mortgage broker or lender. Always identify one property that you control and can absolutely, positively close in 180 days without issues.

With a thorough understanding of the rules and the right team in place, Section 1031 exchanges can feel fairly simple and straightforward, but when details aren't taken care of, the consequences can come back to bite you.

Chapter Eight
Debt

Essentials

A significant amount of time and effort goes into negotiating and closing the mortgage debt, and the importance of this topic is essential to understanding Section 1031 exchanges. You must have the same amount of debt on the replacement property as you had on the relinquished property. If you have no debt on the relinquished property, this rule does not apply–you don't need debt on the replacement property; and you can always take on more debt if you want.

The theory is simple: you are not taxable on borrowed money because you have to pay the debt back with after-tax dollars. If you are relieved of a debt, you will be taxable on the relief of indebtedness–a standard concept in the Tax Code.

Note: taxpayers who want to reduce their debt, or "de-leverage," can repay debt prior to the sale of the relinquished property. They can also de-leverage at closing by bringing cash from another source to closing. Also, adding debt has its benefits as well. Additional debt creates new tax basis that generates depreciation deductions and shelters cash flow from taxation. This will be reviewed in more depth in Chapter 9.

Terminology

"De-leverage": To de-leverage is to reduce debt.

"Loan-to-Value (LTV) Ratio": LTV ratio, or sometimes just "LTV," refers to the relationship between money borrowed (debt) and the full value of the asset.

"Exit LTV": Exit LTV is the loan-to-value ratio when the relinquished property is transferred, which is the amount of debt required on the replacement property for a complete exchange.

In the second scenario of Sally's story, discussed in the prior chapter, the matter of debt was the wrench thrown into the gears. To structure a complete exchange, two things have to happen. People understand the first thing and sometimes struggle with the second.

Starting with the first, think about your old-fashioned settlement statement. At the bottom of the statement, it says "net proceeds to seller." That's the cash proceeds of sale–your equity–that must be reinvested in the replacement property. In this moment at the closing, the seller has an option: you can engage a qualified intermediary to hold the proceeds or cash out. Some cash out and pay the taxes. Many people don't want to pay any taxes, so they engage a qualified intermediary, sign an Exchange Agreement before closing, and choose to have the net proceeds sent to the qualified intermediary to be held in an exchange escrow for their replacement property. To the qualified intermediaries out there, sorry to call you the monkey in the middle, but you are in the middle holding the money. So, you're the monkey in the middle. We've been through this in detail. But that's the first part of Section 1031 exchanges, going through the proper process.

Secondly, if you have debt on your relinquished property, you must have equal or greater debt on your replacement property. People struggle with this one, but it's pretty simple at its core. If you think about it, when you borrow money, there's no tax. Borrow money, and you have to pay it back. When you pay something back, it's after tax, right? So, you borrow money without taxation because you have to pay the debt back with after-tax dollars; if you are relieved of a debt, you will be taxable on the relief of indebtedness, a standard concept in the Tax Code.

Let's return to Sally and the rental property she was selling. For the sake of easy math, let's work with some simple numbers. If she was selling a $100 property, with a 50% loan-to-value (LTV) mortgage, this would mean 50% of the value of the property is borrowed, meaning debt, and the remaining 50% is equity. For a fictional $100 property, this would be

$50 of debt and $50 in equity–assuming no closing costs. Following the rules of a Section 1031 exchange, Sally needs to reinvest the $50 held by her qualified intermediary in qualifying replacement property, and the replacement property needs to be encumbered by a mortgage of $50 or more.

Again, if you want to cash out a portion of the proceeds, you're welcome to pay tax on the portion cashed out. But keep two things in mind. First, you get your tax basis out last, which means the cash will be taxable. And second, the gain usually will be taxed at the highest federal rate due to depreciation recapture (25%) plus state tax. Also, you need to know your exit LTV and be thoughtful about matching or increasing it with debt on your replacement property.

Some people hate debt, but it can be useful. You might not see it that way. Not everyone believes me. I once had a lady in Beverly Hills scream at me.

"We worked all of our lives to get out of debt. Now, we are debt free; we don't want any debt, young man!"

I'm not that young, but she couldn't tell because we were on the phone. She made the choice to de-leverage, meaning she reduced her debt.

She said, "I have money in my Schwab money market account that is just sitting there. I'm going to use that cash to reduce my debt on the real estate." So, she did, and that worked just fine.

I was having the same debt discussion with another property owner who had no debt on her relinquished property either.

She said the same thing, "I don't want no stinkin' debt," in connection with a DST investment.

Some DSTs are all cash, meaning no debt. Most DSTs have debt already in place because most exchangers need debt to satisfy the 1031 debt rule. I explained that DST debt is fully non-recourse, meaning that she was not the borrower and not personally liable to repay the debt. The property is the collateral for the loan.

She was comforted to realize that I was the key principal on the Fannie Mae loan in question. I was the one responsible.

Now, she did not need debt because her relinquished property was debt free. She had a very low tax basis on her relinquished property, and that minimal basis would carry over in her exchange, meaning she would have very little depreciation deductions to shelter her distributions. Said another way, most of her distributions from the replacement property would be subject to federal and state taxes. I explained that this debt would give her new tax basis; new tax basis would create new depreciation deductions that essentially shelter her distributions from taxation. For how long? In many cases, the new basis creates enough new depreciation deductions to shelter the owner's distributions for the entire holding period. In other words, by taking on debt, she will pick up depreciation deductions, increasing her after-tax returns dramatically. She was suddenly much more interested in this tax-free income stream.

Note: we will cover depreciation deductions shortly in Chapter 9.

I have had the debt conversation many, many times; frequently, the property owner elects to take on debt for the tax benefits, and, sometimes, the owner simply "doesn't want no stinkin' debt." The property owner gets to decide what is best in their unique situation, but they should do so after being fully informed of the possibilities.

People struggle with the 1031 debt rule. It shouldn't be that complicated. I tell our investors to call when they have questions. To review what we've covered so far, to obtain complete deferral, the exchanger must do two things: reinvest the net proceeds of sale and have equal (or greater) debt on the replacement property. That's all; it's not so complicated. So, breaking this down:

1. **Reinvest the net proceeds of sale:** The taxpayer must purchase replacement property that is equal to (or greater than) the value of the relinquished property.

- This means reinvesting all of the net proceeds from the relinquished property in qualifying replacement property (like-kind real estate).

- Any cash received will be taxable.

2. **Equal Debt:** If the relinquished property is encumbered by debt, the taxpayer must have equal (or greater) debt on the replacement property. Any reduction in debt is taxable as boot. Taxpayers can de-leverage by prepaying debt prior to closing or bringing cash to closing from another source (not from the exchange) to reduce debt and de-leverage at closing.

And in the end, the taxpayer must not receive anything except like-kind property. Non-like-kind property includes anything else of value received in the exchange. This could be personal property, such as a car or tractor, cash, or even debt reduction.

Keep these two things in mind: you get your tax basis out last, which means the boot will be taxable, and the gain usually will be taxable at the highest federal rate (25%) due to depreciation recapture plus state tax.

Sometimes farmers throw in a tractor "to boot," and the value of that tractor is taxable to the party that receives it. A tractor is not like-kind property in a real estate exchange. If you have something like that, it's best to keep it outside of the exchange. I suggest you work it out some other way. I am fond of old tractors, something like a Ford 8N from the 1940s. They're collectible, so if you don't know what to do with it, feel free to send it over to Hillbrook Farm in Hanover County, Virginia.

Here's another great way to remember how the concept of boot works. One of Capital Square's top selling representatives had an investor who cashed out a few thousand dollars on a taxable basis to buy a horse. Guess what she named the horse? You guessed it: "Boot," not because the owner wore boots but because she cashed out a small portion of her exchange proceeds on a taxable basis.

This leads to another "shaggy dog" story (as we say down South) because Boot was a retired racehorse; he didn't earn enough from the track to pay his hay bill. His original owner sold him to the real estate investor who cashed out the purchase price from her exchange. And guess what she did with Boot? Instead of retiring him or worse, she made him into a three-day eventing horse. As I've mentioned, that's what I do for a hobby. It's from the cavalry, where you have to ride three phases in a competitive horse trial that can span three days: fancy riding called "dressage," jumping obstacles in an arena called "stadium jumping," and my favorite, "cross country jumping," where you have to jump big, scary immovable objects, like ditches and banks, and race through the water in a timed competition.

Boot took to eventing like a duck to water and became very successful with her new owner in the irons. He won his first horse trial at the Virginia Horse Park in Lexington, Virginia, in the fall of 2024 at a competition sponsored by (you guessed it) Capital Square, my firm. Small world, I was there myself, competing on my favorite horse, Brody aka BroDozer. Boot was so successful in his new role that his new owner didn't mind paying a little tax to boot.

The moral of the Boot story: it is more important to accomplish your life goals than worry about paying a little tax. Now, if we are talking about a big tax, there may be a way to cash out without paying the tax. How? Through knowledge about the Tax Code.

Real estate investors are in the saddle, in more ways than one in this case. While deferring taxes is our mantra, there are times when cash is more important than taxes. Boot was worth the modest cost paid in taxes to accomplish the owner's dream of competing in one of the best equestrian venues in the nation (Virginia is horse country). Other exchangers hate debt but have to satisfy Section 1031's debt rule. If they have strong feelings about debt, they can de-leverage, that is, reduce the amount of debt on the replacement property on a taxable basis by taking less debt on the replacement property, as discussed. Receiving some cash or reducing debt may be very important to the exchanger. And read on, because there may be ways to cash out or de-leverage without immediate taxation.

I know this is a book about taxation, but real estate investments are merely tools that should be used to accomplish important goals, usually tax deferral, but sometimes other things. And for the savvy real estate investor, there are ways to cash out or de-leveraging without taxation. That is getting into the deep end of the pool. More on that to come.

Returning to Sally's hypothetical $100 rental property, with $50 debt and $50 of equity, she could make an even exchange if she bought another $100 replacement property with a $50 debt and using her $50 of equity as the downpayment. That's really simple. But investment property does not come in even $100 increments. Let's say she likes a $110 replacement property and wants to trade up. If the bank will loan her $60, she can take that plus her $50 of equity, and it works perfectly. She has to have equal or greater debt. If the bank is now loaning her $60, her debt is more than 50% or $50. That's a good exchange. The $10 debt trade up amount will give her additional tax basis, but we'll get to that in the next chapter.

In the end of this conversation, just remember that 1031 gives you one bite at the apple–tax deferral and not debt forgiveness. If you didn't have to offset that debt with equal or greater debt, you would be getting two bites of the apple, more than your allotted share. That's just not the law. So, reinvest the net proceeds, offset debt with equal or greater debt, and you're done.

Chapter Nine
Tax Consequences, Depreciation & Cost Segregation

Essentials

When you purchase a property, you have a tax basis equal to the cost (purchase price plus closing costs). Tax basis is the metric used to compute depreciation deductions that shelter cash flow from taxation. Also, tax basis is the metric used to compute taxable gain on a sale:

Sales price - closing costs - tax basis = taxable gain.

Tax basis gets lower and lower over time as you depreciate a property. If you have low basis and you do an exchange, your adjusted basis, meaning the original basis less depreciation taken over time, carries over to the replacement property and becomes the new basis of the replacement property. If you trade up to a bigger property, you can increase the basis. Depreciation deductions increase after-tax returns by generating additional after-tax cash flow. Let's say you receive $100 of taxable income. What if the income was sheltered by

$35 of depreciation deductions? Your after-tax return from the property would be increased by $35. Financial assets, such as stocks and bonds, do not qualify for depreciation deductions. Moreover, cost segregation is a tax-planning tool used to accelerate depreciation deductions by allocating costs to shorter-lived assets that qualify for a type of accelerated depreciation called bonus depreciation. We will discuss cost segregation and bonus depreciation below.

Terminology

"Basis": Basis is the metric used to compute depreciation deductions and taxable gain on a sale. The starting basis in a purchase is: purchase price + closing costs = basis. In an exchange, the taxpayer's tax basis in the relinquished property carries over to the replacement property. That basis may be increased if the taxpayer takes on more debt than on the relinquished property or adds cash that is not from the exchange. The taxpayer then uses that basis to compute future depreciation deductions. We refer to this as "adjusted basis" since it has been adjusted (reduced) by prior depreciation deductions.

"Basis of replacement property": This metric is computed as follows: basis of relinquished property–any money received + any gain recognized.

Years ago, my mailman client said to me in a mumbling way, "I want $100,000."

And I said, "What are you talking about?"

"I want $100,000."

"Come on," I repeated. I'd gotten to know him over many lemonades on his front porch at this point.

"What are you talking about?"

"I've never had any money," the mailman finally answered. "I want a box of money. I want to roll around in a box of money, because I've never had any."

I tried to tell him about tax consequences and basis. I hadn't yet gotten to the exciting stuff like depreciation and cost segregation, though I was getting there, but he waved me off. I had introduced him to an experienced CPA and helped him build a team of experts–lawyer, CPA and QI–to help with his exchanges. He called his CPA.

His CPA told him how much it was going to cost in taxes–federal and state–if he truly wanted all that cash to roll around in, and his eyes widened.

After he hung up the phone, he finally said, "I don't actually want $100,000. I'm going to get lots of cash flow from the replacement properties and don't need to pay this big tax." He was becoming smarter and smarter. That mailman was discovering the bigger picture, and that's exactly why I'm writing this book for you. Understanding the intricacies of Section 1031 exchanges can be life changing for you and the generations that follow you–if you ensure you get it right.

So, if you want to partially cash out of an exchange, no problem. It's best to take cash at the beginning, at the front-end closing of the relinquished property. Once the proceeds of sale go into the QI account, as I've said, it might get hung up for 181 days. Exchangers may want to cash out a portion of the sales proceeds for a number of reasons, but remember, the cash received is taxable at the highest rate, while the remainder of the transaction qualifies for exchange treatment. But, before cashing out, exchangers should carefully calculate the tax cost, and they may change their mind the way the mailman did.

In fact, several factors are at play in addition to Section 1031.

Real estate owners are allowed a deduction called "depreciation" that reduces taxable income from their property. This deduction is intended to compensate property owners for wear, tear, and obsolescence. This tax deduction increases after-tax returns from real estate and is not available for financial assets, such as stocks and bonds. It is an amazing fact–real estate tends to appreciate, but we are allowed a deduction for depreciation. Another reason smart people invest in real estate.

Most exchangers have taken depreciation deductions during the time they owned their relinquished property, which has reduced their tax basis. This means that the tax basis that carries over in an exchange is usually relatively low. The upshot: exchangers typically have low basis, which equates to a large gain that has been deferred and will be triggered on a sale. For this reason, exchangers are highly motivated to exchange repeatedly to continue their tax deferral.

Swap till ya' drop in action.

The computation of depreciation has several considerations. To begin, the Tax Reform Act of 1986 introduced the Modified Accelerated Cost Recovery System (MACRS). Under MACRS, a class life is assigned to each asset class, as follows:

Asset Class	Class Life
Nonresidential Real Property	39 years
Residential Real Property	27.5 years
Land Improvements	15 years
Personal Property (affixed to real property)	7 and 5 years

The owner's basis in the property (typically cost plus improvements) is recovered over the assigned class life of the asset. Residential property has a 27.5-year class life, which means that the owner is allowed an annual depreciation deduction computed as follows:

Residential Real Property
cost basis x 1/27.5 per year
= 3.63% depreciation deduction per year

Nonresidential property has a thirty-nine-year class life, which means that the owner is allowed an annual depreciation deduction computed as follows:

Nonresidential Real Property
cost basis x 1/39 per year
= 2.56% depreciation deduction per year

Thinking about how this can look in action, assume a property owner has a $1.1 million cost basis in real estate with a $100,000 land value. The first step is to exclude the $100,000 land value because land is not depreciable (land does not wear out). That gives us some easy math if we're starting this conversation looking at $1 million.

If the property is residential, the owner is entitled to $36,300 per year in depreciation deductions (3.63% depreciation deduction per year). If the property is nonresidential, the owner is entitled to $25,600 per year in depreciation deductions (2.56% depreciation deduction per year). This means that the first $36,300 or $25,600 of rental income will be free of tax. In addition, 100% of the property's cost basis (excluding land value) is recovered over the class life for the asset:

$36,300 per year x 27.5 years = $1 million, the original cost basis and $25,600 per year x 39 years = $1 million, the original cost basis

Depreciation is a "non-cash" tax deduction. Most tax deductions–such as real estate taxes, insurance, maintenance, and repairs–require a cash payment to obtain the deduction. However, depreciation is a non-cash deduction. In other words, the owner does not pay for the deductions, making depreciation all the more valuable.

Depreciation deductions increase after-tax returns from real estate investments by generating additional after-tax cash flow. Financial assets, such as stocks and bonds, do not qualify for depreciation deductions. Also, residential property is depreciated more quickly than nonresidential property (27.5 years versus 39 years, shorter life means quicker recovery). This added tax benefit encourages tax-sensitive investors to focus on residential property. We get to shelter our income from taxation. You don't get that with stocks and bonds. You do get that with real estate. Is it any wonder why some of the wealthiest families have invested in real estate for many generations?

And that's not even the end of the benefits.

Since the Tax Cuts & Jobs Act of 2017, we've been using cost segregation to push these benefits even further. Cost segregation can be a little technical. Think long, boring engineering reports, but they sure are valuable come year end when you're doing your taxes.

The essential information here is that cost segregation allows you to accelerate your depreciation deductions. They assess and analyze the components of a building, breaking the whole down into the assets with a shorter class life. Shorter class life means quicker depreciation deductions. So, rather than a residential asset class life of 27.5 years, we look at various components of that total asset. Some, such as personal property, are five years.

Some, such as land improvements, are fifteen. This means a taxpayer is able to depreciate a portion of the replacement property using a shorter personal property recovery period and not the longer recovery period generally applicable to real property.

By breaking a building down into these components, you're able to accelerate the depreciation deductions. One recent example is a multifamily community that Capital Square sponsored as a DST in Richmond, Virginia. By breaking the building down into components, including the clubhouse, the apartment units, the grilling pavilion, and the pool, the cost segregation study concluded that an investor in this property may claim a deduction of 8.1%, instead of 3.63%, in the year of acquisition. Thus, our investors were able to accelerate their depreciation deductions and have more after-tax income. That is an additional benefit: a tax deduction today that creates additional after-tax cash flow. This is referred to as the time value of money.

This is a complex subject, so let's spend a little more time here: how does cost segregation actually work?

The property owner engages a qualified engineering firm to prepare a cost segregation study that allocates their cost basis for the property into the class lives shown above. The goal is to increase the allocation to the shorter-lived assets that qualify for bonus depreciation:

| Land Improvements | 15 years |
| Personal Property (Affixed to Real Property) | 7 and 5 years |

Thus, cost segregation studies highlight where bonus depreciation can come into play, accelerating depreciation deductions. Assets with a MACRS recovery life of twenty years or fewer qualify for bonus depreciation.

Interestingly, the Tax Cuts & Jobs Act of 2017 increased the bonus depreciation percentage to 100% for assets placed in service by December 31, 2022; 80% by December 31, 2023; 60% by December 31, 2024; and 40% by December 31, 2025. This last date is when the Act was designed to expire, though at the time of this writing, there is talk in D.C. about extending key provisions.

So, in the end here, allocating to shorter-lived assets with a cost segregation study can dramatically accelerate depreciation deductions. This will increase after-tax returns by generating additional cash flow.

At Capital Square, all DST offerings come with a cost segregation study. We have some investors who invest in DSTs to get excess losses to shelter their income from other real estate investments. Some want to take a little cash, but it would be taxable. They're using bonus depreciation to generate excess losses at closing, so they can cash out a little and avoid paying any tax because of these excess losses. That's the value of depreciation.

What do I mean by reducing boot and cashing out at closing? Well, as we've covered, depreciation deductions reduce taxable income from real estate. This means that bonus depreciation deductions can be used to offset taxable gain from real estate.

Under Section 1031, any cash received or reduction in liabilities will be taxable as boot. **Bonus depreciation deductions can be used to offset Section 1031 boot. This can be boot from cash received, liabilities reduced, or a non-like-kind property received.** In this way, taxpayers can use bonus depreciation to cash out of an exchange or reduce liabilities without gain recognition. This is an excellent strategy for exchangers who would like some cash out of an exchange or to de-leverage.

Note: the cost segregation study only impacts depreciation deductions, not the qualification of the transaction as a Section 1031 exchange.

To recap, using cost segregation in this manner can dramatically accelerate (increase) depreciation deductions, increasing the after-tax returns for real estate investments.

Using bonus depreciation can generate enough excess depreciation deductions to reduce or eliminate taxable gain on boot.

If you're feeling unsure about any of this, remember that you should always work with trusted professional partners. After a CPA verifies the numbers, they too will embrace the potential of tax deferrals through Section 1031 exchanges, recognizing the proper uses of depreciation deductions and cost segregation studies. They're CPAs. Of course they will verify the numbers and process. That's their job. They should do it. And after they do their job, you should feel confident about the tax consequences and your tax-deferral. Remember that deferral can become as permanent as you want it to be, if you hang onto the replacement property and structure future sales as 1031 exchanges. Technically, it's just deferral, as your CPA will remind you. However, knowing the opportunities of "swap till ya' drop" is a wealth-building change-maker.

What is the origin of the term "boot"? Good question.

Its story goes all the way back to Old English, where the word *bōt* meant compensation or advantage. It makes me very happy to know that Section 1031 is mentioned in the definition of "boot" on Merriam-Webster Dictionary's website.

Now, let's jump past Old English and Middle English all the way back to the modern day. Around the time when Section 1031 was originally adopted, it is thought that two farmers were exchanging their real estate. This was an old school, property-for-property simultaneous exchange in which farmer A exchanged lot A with farmer B for lot B. Farmer A threw in an old tractor "to boot" to even up the values.

The concept of boot has been around for a long time. The old word and the old style of exchanging both feel like a long time ago. Today, the exchange would likely have been structured as a deferred exchange with a qualified intermediary to obtain the benefit of the safe harbor discussed in Chapter 5.

Now, if you receive non-like-kind property—whether a tractor, furniture, or the horses in the barn—the recipient will be taxable based on the value of the property received. Some things never change, like a good old pair of work boots, which is a different type of boot, but there you go.

Just wait. My favorite pathway for "swap till ya' drop" legacy building is coming up next.

Chapter Ten
Delaware Statutory Trusts (DSTs)

The Essentials

A Delaware statutory trust (DST) is a legal entity formed under Delaware law that qualifies as like-kind real estate for purposes of Section 1031. The DST structure allows investors to participate in a Section 1031 exchange and receive passive income as well as potential for appreciation from real estate ownership. This equation provides the potential for superior after-tax returns that real estate owners can use to create generational wealth.

DSTs are promoted by real estate firms, known as "sponsors," responsible for everything on a turn-key basis. The sponsor acquires the real estate, typically places the debt (because most exchangers need debt), manages the property over an established holding period (typically seven to ten years), and ultimately sells the property by the end of the holding period with the proceeds returned to the DST owners (most of whom will do another exchange). Investment programs like this with a sponsor are sometimes referred to as "syndicated," because the sponsor typically arranges a syndicate of broker-dealers and investment advisors to sell the offering to investors.

A Delaware statutory trust is referred to as "fractionalized" ownership because each DST owner owns a fraction–a percentage–of the DST's property. This is compared to a "whole" property, where the investor owns 100% of the property.

In the DST structure, the DST owns 100% of the real estate. The investors own interests in the DST, technically referred to as "beneficial interests," and as you will see, DSTs qualify for Section 1031 exchange treatment if structured properly to comply with IRS requirements. The sponsor serves as the "signatory trustee" with the sole power and authority to make decisions for the DST, including sale of the property. The DST also has a Delaware trustee to satisfy statutory requirements.

To qualify for exchange treatment, DSTs must satisfy a number of strict requirements set forth in Revenue Ruling 2004-86. This includes being a fixed investment trust, in which the beneficial owners are passive. If the real estate is active, for example, an apartment community, the sponsor must master lease the property from the beneficial owners. So, the sponsor is active, and the investors are passive. This is not required if the real estate is already passive–for example, if it is net leased. (More discussions of net leases and gross leases are in Chapter 13.)

Further Details & Benefits

A DST is a distinct legal entity formed in Delaware, a state well known for business-friendly laws and reliable courts. The DST structure is exceptionally flexible and can be used in a variety of circumstances–for example, to operate a business, create an estate plan, or to own real estate.

By using a DST, the owner has the benefit of a modern statute with off-the-shelf rules that include limited liability, asset protection, and confidentiality. The taxation of DSTs is equally flexible; a DST can be taxed as a partnership, corporation, or trust.

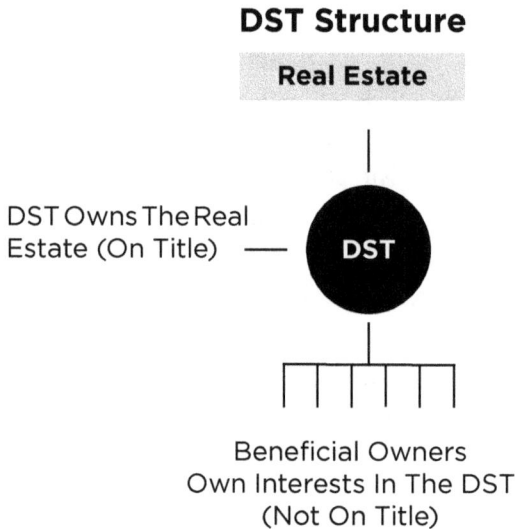

DST Structure

Real Estate

DST Owns The Real Estate (On Title) — **DST**

Beneficial Owners
Own Interests In The DST
(Not On Title)

In our case, DSTs are used in a unique way: as the entity that owns the replacement property for fractionalized Section 1031 exchange programs. When we talk about DSTs throughout this book, we are talking about DSTs that satisfy the Revenue Ruling to qualify as replacement property for purposes of Section 1031.

Key features of a DST:

- Investors have no personal liability.
- Investors do not submit loan applications or sign loan documents.
- A lower investment minimum means that a greater number of investors can participate.
- With such a low minimum (typically $50,000 per DST investment), investors can diversify by acquiring a number of DST replacement properties.
- The simple investment process is streamlined and accessible.
- All of the due diligence is complete and available in an electronic drop box.
- The sponsor manages the property and makes decisions for the DST.

DSTs are not liquid like stocks and bonds, because there is no trading market for them. To be clear, you can transfer them–for example, you can sell a DST–but there is no trading market like the New York Stock Exchange. Liquidity comes when the DST property is sold and the sales proceeds are returned to DST owners. There is no interim liquidity.

When is a DST property sold? Typically, between years seven and ten. This requires some explanation because DST tax rules require sale of the property when the loan matures. Most DST loans have a term of ten years, which means that most DST properties must be sold within ten years. However, Capital Square has been selling DST properties much quicker–going full-cycle in fewer than five years in many cases when DST properties have appreciated to the point where a sale is in the investors' best interests. Most owners will reinvest their original capital and profits by 1031 exchanging into another DST to continue the tax deferral.

An increasing number of exchangers consider DSTs for their replacement property.

Why?

Many want a passive replacement property that complies with the requirements of Section 1031 after selling a property that is management intensive. They are drawn to the DST structure because a reputable sponsor provides all the services on a turn-key basis, with properties structured to provide stable cash flow and capital appreciation without the headaches associated with toilets, tenants, trash, and the occasional teenager. Others have non-income-producing property, for example land, and acquire a DST replacement property to generate cash flow.

The IRS issued a Revenue Ruling in 2004 (Rev. Rul. 2004-86) describing how to properly structure a DST to qualify for Section 1031 exchange treatment. Now we know that a properly structured DST interest qualifies as like-kind replacement property in a Section 1031 exchange, just like a whole property. That is a published ruling with the status of law. Did you know the IRS issues private letter rulings upon the request of taxpayers seeking guidance on specific tax issues? Private letter rulings are not binding on other taxpayers, but published rulings are a statement of law and are binding on all taxpayers.

Note: a Delaware statutory trust is not a "trust" as that term is commonly used to create a fiduciary relationship, for example, in a will or trust; a DST is an ownership vehicle used in this case to create 1031 exchange programs.

The background of Section 1031 as well as the history of Tenants in Common (TIC), which will be discussed in Chapter 11, are both important to our discussion. But for now, know that starting around 2012, when the U.S. economy was in recovery from the Great Financial Crisis of 2008, the DST structure took hold and has become the structure of choice for fractionalized exchange programs. As the awareness of DSTs increases, a growing number of exchangers start with DSTs in their hunt for replacement property, while others use DSTs as a backup on their list of identified properties.

DSTs are a unique form of "fractionalized" real estate ownership, meaning each DST owner essentially owns a fraction of the DST's property. For example, if you own 5% of the DST, you own 5% of the DST's real estate, along with 5% of its income and expenses. In short, you own 5% of the DST and all of its attributes.

Compare this to typical real estate ownership, where the title holder owns 100% of the property, the entire or "whole" property, whether the whole duplex, the whole beach house, or whatever the whole property may be. With DSTs, we're only talking about owning a percentage of the property, which opens up a number of interesting possibilities.

Benefits of Delaware Statutory Trusts

1. Tax advantages of a Section 1031 exchange
2. Access to investment-grade real estate a taxpayer would not otherwise be able to afford on their own

3. The ability to diversify into multiple replacement properties to reduce risk
4. Lower minimum investment than a whole property
5. A largely automated, simplified closing process
6. An existing pipeline of qualifying replacement properties where due diligence has already been completed
7. Debt in place (non-recourse) for exchangers who need debt to qualify for exchange treatment
8. Liability protection and confidentiality

Looking at each of these ideas one by one, we return to the tax advantages. By this point, you know the value of Section 1031 exchanges, and DSTs are one straightforward pathway to making a successful exchange. You'll defer the taxes; those include recapture taxes on prior depreciation at 25%, the federal capital gains taxes of up to 20%, and the 3.8% add-on for the Affordable Care Act if you are a high-bracket taxpayer, plus capital gains taxes at the state level (unless you live in a state without an income tax). That is a lot of taxes being deferred.

You recall that Section 1031 doesn't forgive taxes. It defers them. But again, you have the control. Thus, every time you want to sell, you say, "Do I want to pay the tax? No, I don't. I'll do another exchange."

Every time, you can keep deferring and deferring and deferring the tax. This is how you build family wealth over time. The taxes that would have been paid are instead invested in replacement property of your choosing, compounding your wealth in real estate. So, there's DST benefit number one–Section 1031 exchange treatment.

Then there's the powerful benefit of accessing higher quality real estate that an owner would not otherwise be able to afford on their own. Section 1031 requires "like-kind property," which as we know means any kind of real estate. You might have a rental house, but with the Delaware statutory trust, you can reinvest your proceeds into a portion of a large investment-grade property, much higher quality than your lovely little rental. You can invest as little as $50,000 in a DST that owns a $100 million property, the best property in that submarket, with the best tenants and the best managers–all that on a turn-key basis. You could never own a property of that magnitude on your own. DSTs are amazing!

The sponsors of DST properties tend to be large real estate companies. My firm, Capital Square, has over 350 employees and all the bells and whistles that are used to improve property ownership, management, and operations, along with an expert team that handles acquisitions, legal matters, financing, accounting, investor relations, asset management, and property management–the whole nine yards. A small owner could never afford all of that. Additionally, at Capital Square, we aim to purchase real estate at approximately 5–10% below appraised value and to lock in fixed-interest-rate debt at a very favorable rate through our extensive lender relationships. It would be very hard for a mom-and-pop owner/operator to replicate.

Plus, with DSTs, you can diversify. Instead of acquiring one property as your replacement property, you can reinvest your proceeds into several replacement properties, reducing the risk of having your investment concentrated in a single asset. We learned from the Great Financial Crisis of 2008 not to overly concentrate exchangers into a single property. We aim to diversify whenever possible into several properties, and larger exchangers can diversify into a large portfolio of DST replacement properties. It's like building your own real estate investment fund. In short, things happen. Diversify to reduce risk.

Nobody believed that General Motors would go bankrupt in 2007. How many companies have gone bad over the years? Roughly half the companies that were on the New York Stock Exchange in the year 2000 are no longer on the stock exchange.[vi] Those were big companies. What we've learned from all this and from the Great Financial Crisis of 2008 is to diversify. Don't put too many eggs in one basket.

Also, investing into multiple DSTs will allow you to invest 100% of your exchange proceeds. Compare that to whole properties that are likely too big or too small to fit your precise needs. Let's say you have $179,500 of exchange proceeds. You can invest exactly that $179,500, no more and no less, in DSTs. If a whole property costs $200,000, that would be too big as a replacement property. You would have to come up with additional cash. If a whole property was $150,000, that would be too small. You would have taxable boot on the leftover funds. **DSTs remind me of Goldilocks; DSTs are just right.**

Not to mention the 1031 debt rule that requires you to have equal debt on your replacement property. DSTs typically come with debt in place to satisfy the 1031 debt rule.

Because DSTs have a small minimum investment, someone with even a modest amount of proceeds from their exchange can go into two or three DSTs; a larger investor can go into four or more DSTs. Then if something unexpected happens, you still have the others to fall back on.

With a minimum investment of $50,000 per DST, if a taxpayer has $200,000 from a relinquished property that was a duplex, they might say, "This is great. I want to put $50,000 in four different DST properties. I want to diversify to reduce my risk."

They couldn't buy four properties on their own if they wanted to for $200,000. But they can buy several different DSTs because these higher-quality, investment-grade properties are available and easily accessible with a low minimum investment. They are all right there, ready to go.

So, diversify to reduce risk, and then swap till ya' drop, building family wealth over the decades. When your heirs get the step up in basis, they can sell, and the tax is essentially forgiven. If you're big enough, you may have an estate tax, but your heirs will inherit a tax basis that is equal to the fair market value. Yes, it's a shame that we have to die for them to get that benefit, but there's no free lunch for you or for me. (Although, you'll discover in Chapter 14 that with qualified opportunity zone funds, you don't always have to die to get tax forgiveness).

Another detail to note is that tax rules require the sale of DST properties when their loans mature. Most loans have a ten-year term, and so, come ten years, every DST property that has debt must be sold. But this is not the end of the world. You can do another exchange. Swap till ya' drop. It's a tax-advantaged, wealth-building mantra for a reason.

Properties generally appreciate. Cash flow grows over time, and then at the end of the rainbow, most exchangers with Capital Square have exchanged again and again into another DST program sponsored by Capital Square, building family wealth over time. Serial exchangers, remember? I don't call them that because they eat Cheerios.

Most just keep exchanging, except those that have passed, but they don't need to. They've achieved tax forgiveness and greater wealth for their heirs.

Another positive aspect of investing in DSTs is that you'll be working with a reputable real estate firm, like my own, that specializes in 1031 exchanges and DSTs. You don't have to assemble your own team of specialists to ensure you get it right, because the team is already assembled. Typically, with DSTs, you're also working with an experienced financial advisor or registered representative, and that is helpful along with the largely automated, simplified exchange process that is already in place. It's already been in practice for thousands of exchangers. There's comfort in experience and proven proficiency.

Moreover, because DST sponsors are mostly large firms like Capital Square, existing pipelines of qualifying replacement properties where due diligence has already been completed are often at the ready, no matter a taxpayer's timeline. For example, Capital Square buys DST properties in advance of investor needs. Most DSTs have debt in place for exchangers who need debt to qualify for exchange treatment. Then, when a DST financial advisor drops by or gets in touch and they say, "I want to see everything," we'll respond, "Great. Here are five or more options that are available right now."

After a conversation about different asset classes and debt structures to fit the investor's needs, we discuss the benefits and risks of each property. Then, when the time comes to discuss the due diligence, we'll continue, "Here's the password to our electronic drop box. For DSTs, you can see the title, survey, environmental report, property condition report, roof report, business plan, loan documents, risk factors, and much more."

In short, everything an investor will want to see and know is there and available immediately, including a disclosure document called a Private Placement Memorandum (PPM) and a cost segregation study for exchangers who want bonus depreciation (as discussed in Chapter 9). The closing documents can be easily signed and returned on your smartphone—no need to attend the closing.

After closing, all of the investor's documents are loaded into a secure investor portal. If an investor can't sleep at night, they can log in 24/7, anytime they want to see the latest financials and property updates. The goal is fewer sleepless nights during the exchange process and after the DST is owned. And with DSTs, you don't run the risk of not having a property when the clock ticks by and you're out of days on the calendar.

The house flippers will put three houses down on their identification list, and then they'll call at the last minute and say, "You know, one of them had a problem, and the other two were sold out from under me. I ended up with nothing."

It's a real concern. There's not always a desirable "whole" replacement property for you at the required time, so lately, a lot of exchangers have been identifying DSTs as a backup. They put one of Capital Square's DSTs on their identification list, usually a large property that will be available for a long time. (DSTs are offered to investors until the offering is sold out; larger offerings of $50 million or more take much longer to fully subscribe, so they are excellent candidates for backup identifications that could hang out for the exchanger's entire 180-day closing period.)

Exchangers often say, "Oh, it's an emergency backup. I'll just put a DST on the ID list so I don't get stuck having to pay the tax if I can't find anything." And then they call when the other identified properties fall out, or when they continue their research and realize the value of the DST property.

But wait, there's more, as they used to say on late-night TV ads. **Liability protection is another huge win with DSTs.** You have no personal liability under Delaware law, and the debt is non-recourse. You're not liable for the debt. You don't have to fill out a loan application. You don't have to do anything for the lender. Your property is what's encumbered by a mortgage. Your investment is at risk for that debt, but you're not personally liable for it. In addition, your personal assets are protected from liability to the DST's creditors or the creditors of other investors.

Liability from real estate activities is a very big deal. Back in the day, only corporations provided liability protection. Over the years, limited partnerships and, since the mid-1990s, limited liability companies (LLCs) have been used for liability protection. However, this is not needed with a DST because Delaware law automatically provides limited liability along with other benefits, including asset protection and confidentiality. Also, you may recall the 1031 vesting rule: the same taxpayer that owned the relinquished property must acquire the replacement property. If that entity is a partnership for tax purposes, it may be possible to liquidate the entity a year or two after investing in a DST and save the annual filing fees and other costs.

Additionally, DST loans are "non-recourse" to the investors, meaning the property serves as collateral for the loan, and the DST owners are not personally liable for repayment. This structure permits sponsors to create debt to satisfy the Section 1031 debt requirement without subjecting investors to personal liability.

Even when you go into a DST in your own name–as Section 1031 exchange rules require if you're selling your relinquished property in your own name–your name never goes on the title. The DST's name is on title. So, there's another benefit: DST investments are confidential. Your name won't appear in any public records. How great is that?

The sponsor is responsible for compliance with the loan documents and for any so-called "bad boy" carve-out guaranties that create personal liability. "Carve-out guaranties" are used to guarantee the lender against certain bad acts that could harm the lender's collateral, for example, theft of rents or misappropriation of casualty or condemnation awards. By serving as the carve-out guarantor, the sponsor is responsible for protecting the lender against bad acts.

I have the distinction of being the key principal on over sixty loans with Fannie Mae and the carve-out guarantor on over 120 loans overall. It's a long addendum to my personal financial statement. But in short, the lenders look to the DST property and to me, not the investors, if there are issues. That is a very good thing for investors.

It was not always the case. Back in the early days, many lenders would not loan on a DST. Capital Square worked for years with our lending relationships at Walker & Dunlop to become the first sponsor approved by Fannie Mae for a DST loan, the first DST to assume a Freddy Mac loan, the first DST to borrow from several household-name life insurance companies, and more and more. Relationships are vitally important. Walker & Dunlop has done an exceptional job of educating the agency lenders on the virtues of DSTs, helping Capital Square become a top-tier borrower. Thank you, Walker & Dunlop, for believing in Capital Square and helping us along the way.

I will add that a DST is a "grantor trust" for tax purposes. In essence, each owner is treated as owning an undivided interest in the DST's real estate. As noted, if you own 5% of the DST, you own 5% of the DST's real estate, along with 5% of its income and expenses. We're talking all of its attributes–"chicken, guts, and feathers," as they say in Texas. It's funny what you learn traveling the nation, giving tax seminars and being in the real estate business.

There's usually steady cash flow from DSTs as well, because rent is being collected. As an owner of that property, you not only have an investment that will likely appreciate over time; you also have an investment with cash flow that typically grows over time.

In conclusion, DSTs have a low minimum investment and are offered on a turn-key basis, making DSTs accessible to a larger number of exchangers. In addition, DST properties typically are investment-grade real estate that most exchangers could not afford to purchase on their own. DSTs give smaller investors (regular folks) the ability to own some of the highest quality real estate managed by some of the best real estate firms in the nation.

Delaware statutory trusts are the entity Capital Square uses to take a big building–an apartment community, medical building, or industrial warehouse–and to financially break it down into smaller pieces for exchange investors. Most people don't have $100 million or even $25 million to buy such a substantial asset. Thinking about an Amazon facility that Capital Square bought a few years back, it was a third of a billion dollars. Side note: my firm's just thirteen years old, as of the writing of this book, so statements like that still sometimes shock me.

But think about a third of a billion for one property. The beauty of the DST is that an investor could own a little piece of an Amazon sortation facility that moves one million packages a day. It's full of packages, people, and robots. It's 2,690,000 square feet. Have you ever been in a million square foot warehouse? It's scary. You could get lost in there; a golf cart is a necessity. Over two million square feet of space, sitting on 169 acres, leased for decades by one of the largest companies in the world–I've never seen anything like it.

When it was an open offering, you could have invested in this Amazon facility for the princely sum of $50,000 or more. It was purchased with a high debt structure for people who needed debt for their exchange. We've talked about debt. It's an important piece of the puzzle. Most exchangers have a modest level of debt on their relinquished property and only need the same modest amount of debt on their replacement property. DSTs typically have what is known as "low leverage," that is debt of only about 40% to 55%. But some exchangers need much higher debt. This can occur when owners intentionally incur a high level of debt or inadvertently, when the value of their property declines but the debt remains the same. For example, a $100 property with $50 of debt equals a 50% loan to value (LTV); but if the property drops in value to $70, the LTV jumps to over 71%. A "high-leverage" DST is intended to help investors who have higher than normal debt on their relinquished property. They need high LTV to satisfy the 1031 debt rule.

DSTs can be used with any asset class you like. Capital Square has years of experience with medical and industrial properties on triple net leases, but these days, we prefer housing investments because housing is a necessity in short supply, also with exceptional debt options from Fannie Mae and numerous life insurance companies. We put debt on the DST properties to line up with your debt requirements to fully satisfy Section 1031. In this way, we are a solution for exchangers by satisfying their debt requirement. Most people have modest debt on their relinquished property, but if you have a higher debt need, you may require something like that Amazon facility. Thus, DSTs come with different LTVs; we also have all-cash DSTs with no debt. DSTs run the gamut.

Now, I always think back to that lady who yelled at me and said, "I don't want no stinkin' debt, young man." The debt at the time had an interest rate of 3.5%. When we showed her our Fannie Mae loan, she changed her tune.

"Your property makes six percent," she said. "Boy, that's positive leverage. I want some of that."

In addition, she had a very low basis in her relinquished property from decades of depreciation deductions. By exchanging out of her all-cash (no debt) relinquished property into a DST with modest debt, she obtained new tax basis. Bottom line: she was able to shelter her property distributions from federal and state taxation for the entire holding period. She sure changed her depression mentality about debt always being a negative.

And that was after yelling at me.

But for that lady and for the thousands of other investors I've worked with, understanding the potential of Section 1031 exchanges and Delaware statutory trusts was a game-changer. I know that navigating the complex tax rules of a Section 1031 exchange can feel complicated. My goal–and my team's goal–is to simplify and streamline the process so that more investors can enjoy the benefits of Section 1031 via DST ownership. Enabling the discovery and implementation of tax-advantaged real estate investment is how we all build something bigger than ourselves.

Chapter Eleven

Theories of DST vs. Tenants in Common (TIC)

Essentials

The fractionalized real estate landscape has been defined by two significant investment vehicles, first tenants in common (TIC) and, later, the Delaware statutory trust (DST). As a lawyer, I was a part of the movement to commercialize the 1031 industry using the TIC structure and, then, the DST structure as a sponsor at Capital Square. For many reasons, the TIC structure is now essentially obsolete for syndicated exchange programs, but exchangers need not worry. The DST structure has taken its place and is much better.

Why? The DST structure has the most important feature of the TIC structure–tax deferral under Section 1031–without the negative aspects.

Tenants in Common (TIC) structure:

- Rev. Proc. 2002-22 (technically, an advance ruling guideline, not substantive law)
- Following the Great Financial Crisis of 2008, TICs became problematic when the economy crashed; they are now out of favor for syndicated offerings.

Delaware Statutory Trust (DST) structure:

- Rev. Rul. 2004-86 (statement of substantive law)
- DSTs are now the structure of choice.

See Appendix H for a detailed TIC vs. DST comparison.

A t Capital Square, one of our favorite features of DSTs is the ability to diversify into multiple properties to reduce risk. The PhDs who write formal papers on investment risk talk about "not putting all your eggs in one basket." It's kind of folksy, you know? These highly awarded professors with lots of advanced degrees talking about somebody carrying a basket full of eggs. But I like it. It's nice and clear. If you drop the basket, what happens? You break all the eggs. So, the award-winning professors tell us to diversify to reduce risk. Spread your eggs out into many baskets...eh...properties.

Maybe it's hard to think about money in baskets, but I will say this: diversifying your investments is a smart financial strategy. We all know this. However, when it comes to real estate, properties don't come in convenient sizes. Spreading your investments across multiple properties sounds great in theory but is not feasible in the real world of whole properties. DSTs have a low minimum investment per property. Even an exchanger with a modest amount of proceeds can diversify into several DSTs. That way, you're not financially concentrated in a single property. If one basket drops, all your eggs won't shatter.

Also, when buying whole properties, it is easy to go over or under the amount needed for your exchange, while DSTs can be purchased in just the right amount to precisely meet your exchange needs. DSTs permit exchangers to reinvest the very last dollar in qualifying replacement property. Try doing that with whole properties. Keep in mind that any excess funds cashed out will be taxable, usually at the highest rate, while you can invest the very last dollar in DST properties.

We've talked about the advantages of fractionalized real estate ownership. Being able to access higher quality real estate is a dramatic benefit. Imagine going from maintaining a house that you were renting to a school teacher to having fractional ownership of an Amazon sortation facility. You've gone from a school teacher tenant to Amazon, one of the wealthiest companies in the world. That's a powerful trade up in terms of the quality of your property and the financial strength of your tenant.

All this being said, DSTs are the second evolution of the fractionalized ownership model of real estate investing. Beginning in 1990, we started developing what became known as the Tenant in Common (TIC) structure. We had been doing Section 1031 exchanges for quite a long time; we'd been doing real estate investment trusts (REITs), which we'll discuss more in Chapter 15; we'd been doing real estate funds of various types. We knew how to structure real estate investments. But there was no recognized way to take a big building and break it down into smaller pieces that qualified for Section 1031 exchange treatment, until this time. This was kind of earth shattering, groundbreaking actually.

This TIC structure was initially documented by Darryl Steinhause, a lawyer working on behalf of Passco Companies, and me, as outside counsel to Triple Net Properties, LLC (a Virginia limited liability company). Both Passco and Triple Net were based in Orange County, California; both had founders and CEOs who previously ran a real estate company together and had a vision for commercializing real estate via securities broker-dealers to permit small exchangers to enjoy the benefits of turn-key investing in higher quality real estate. Darryl did the original heavy lifting on the structure as counsel to Passco. Then, on behalf of Triple Net Properties, we refined the structure with our team from the Hirschler Fleischer law firm—including Jeff Gregor, Capital Square's current chief legal officer—making the structure work even better.

We called it "Tenants in Common" (TIC), based on the English common law concept. We built TICs to be an investment program that would pass muster with broker-dealers nationwide. Before that, exchangers who wanted 1031 replacement property typically had to find a realtor and acquire a whole property. But with the TIC structure, exchangers were able to acquire a fractionalized interest in a higher quality property on a turn-key basis. This allowed regular folks to exchange into investment-grade real estate that they could not afford on their own. As I said, it was groundbreaking.

We helped to commercialize this new structure by broker-dealers across the nation, and the sale of TICs exploded from zero to billions of dollars in a few short years, as you will see.

TICs were sold by securities broker-dealers and their registered representatives. To understand the playing field, it will help to understand the structure of the securities business. First, broker-dealers are licensed to sell securities by FINRA, a self-regulatory organization that provides a large body of rules and regulations designed to protect the investing public. Broker-dealers hire licensed individuals, called registered representatives, to sell securities to investors and earn a commission on the sale.

There are two types of securities offerings: public and private. All public securities offerings must be registered with the Securities and Exchange Commission (SEC), and private securities offerings must qualify for an exemption. Securities registration with the SEC is frightfully expensive, time-consuming, and not practical for most real estate offerings. Real estate funds typically qualify for an exemption from securities registration under what is known as SEC Reg D. It was not practical to register TIC offerings with the SEC, but there was precedent for exempting TICs under Reg D, just like many private real estate funds and REITs. So, we structured TICs as Reg D private placements for sale by broker-dealers and their registered representatives. And the hook: a securities commission was paid on the sale of TICs. That created a strong incentive in the securities world to learn the new TIC structure, and the broker-dealers already had the resources and systems in place to sell private placements. So, off we went, from ground zero to billions in TIC sales, enlisting an existing army of licensed salespersons nationwide.

A couple of nice benefits resulted from selling TICs as securities through the broker-dealer network. First, broker-dealers are obligated to conduct an independent due diligence investigation on each sponsor and offering. This resulted in strict underwriting of TIC sponsors and offerings, with the ultimate goal of protecting investors. Also, FINRA rules require broker-dealers to determine that each offering is suitable for investors and investors are not being exposed to undue risk, for example, from over-concentration in a particular type of investment. And investors had an effective remedy for breaches by the sales force. FINRA arbitration is a forum for unhappy investors seeking redress from broker-dealers who sold them securities. In conclusion, we plugged the TIC investment into a system of compliance designed to protect investors.

Now, I was a tax lawyer, but it was imperative to understand the securities business to promote the TIC structure. So, off I went to learn securities laws and how that would impact our new investment vehicle. This was not the only new learning experience. I had to learn the real estate business along the way, because real estate is fundamental to Section 1031; the lending business, because debt is critical to most exchanges; and corporate law, because many of the legal entities we use rely on corporate and business law. I haven't even mentioned being licensed by FINRA to sell securities, supervise registered representatives, and manage a broker-dealer. It made my head hurt; I had to learn a lot and quickly.

With the TIC structure, we took real estate for Section 1031 tax purposes and made it into a security for securities law purposes. The law firms structuring TIC offerings gave "should qualify" tax opinions, so we were confident that the structure worked for tax purposes. It was the beginning of what became a huge industry. Soon thereafter, billions of dollars of exchange proceeds were invested in real estate using the TIC structure. It worked perfectly well until the Great Financial Crisis of 2008 essentially killed real estate.

And it started with just two of us: Darryl Steinhause for Passco Capital and me at the Hirschler Fleischer law firm in Richmond, Virginia for Triple Net with its headquarters in Orange County, California. At Hirschler Fleischer, I led a real estate securities practice group, an interdisciplinary group of lawyers dedicated to developing the TIC structure along with REITs and real estate funds. Over time, others became actively involved and helped to create this new industry. Arnie Harrison, a lawyer in Chicago, helped lay the groundwork with his research on land trusts. Then, Triple Net launched its first TIC on a national basis via broker-dealers in 1991; Passco, Inland, and others followed with billions of dollars of TIC offerings. Well done, Daryll and team at Hirschler Fleischer! So, now you know the history.

However, in time, small issues arose with the structure. For example, the names of all the investors were on the Tenants in Common Agreement recorded in the land records. We didn't like that. We wanted our investors to be confidential. Because they wanted their privacy too, we redesigned the documentation to permit the sponsor's officers to sign for the investors, so they wouldn't have to be visible in the land record; that got us confidentiality.

Next, we were concerned that the investors were on the title, which created the real risk of personal liability. To avoid personal liability, we began to use special purpose entities, single-member LLCs, for each TIC investor. These entities are disregarded for tax purposes, and they had recently been approved by the IRS. While the IRS disregarded single-member LLCs, they still gave investors complete liability protection. So, we formed about a million of them, first using Virginia LLCs—and that feels like only a slight exaggeration. Later, the rating agencies for lenders insisted on Delaware, so we formed a very large number of Delaware LLCs for exchangers investing in TIC properties.

That got us pretty far, but the lenders still were not happy. They wanted us to be "bankruptcy remote," meaning structured to minimize the risk of bankruptcy and to isolate financial risk. And so, we went into another round of special purpose entities that were bankruptcy remote. Finally, the rating agencies approved, and TICs became an approved borrower. Then, a new type of lender with a new type of loan, known as a Commercial

Mortgage-Backed Security (CMBS), began to loan on properties using the TIC structure.

Many believe the 2002 Revenue Procedure is the reason the TIC industry took off from 2002 to 2008. They are only partially correct. It was the advent of lending–in particular, CMBS lending–to TIC properties that helped commercialize the TIC structure. Without the debt, we couldn't create viable exchange programs because of the 1031 debt requirement. The Revenue Procedure was a major catalyst, but without debt, there would not have been a TIC industry.

I recall a trip to New York City to meet the CMBS lenders and discuss TIC lending; they were mostly uninterested. The structure was too new and too problematic: a large number of TIC borrowers who don't know each other, having varying degrees of real estate experience, are supposed to own a large property together. What if there was a disagreement? Who would the lender notify if there were problems? What if one of the TIC borrowers had creditors or filed for bankruptcy? Over time, these issues were all resolved, and CMBS became the predominant lender for TIC programs.

So, we had the structure, Steinhause and me (with help from Jeff Gregor and others at the Hirschler Fleischer law firm). We had potential exchange investors, and then eventually we had the CMBS lenders who came on board. Without the loans, we would not have an industry because most exchangers must have debt to satisfy the 1031 debt rule. They must have debt equal to the debt on their relinquished property, as we've discussed. If we couldn't offer them debt, we wouldn't have a viable program.

Here is the interesting part, little known even in the industry. We could have carried on perfectly well with our TIC structure, using tax opinions from national law firms, even without the Revenue Procedure, but we could not have done it without the debt–we would not have an industry because most exchangers must have debt. So, until the CMBS lenders were able to get the rating agencies on board, we had a concept but not the ability to execute broadly. It wasn't the IRS that we needed; it was the lenders. It's one of those little-known facts. So, now you know the inside story.

The TIC programs kept getting refined over time based on what was required to satisfy the rating agencies for CMBS debt. But at the beginning, it was Steinhause and me, and eventually with Tom Jahncke of Passco Capital; Mark Kosanke, founding partner of Concorde Financial Group; Greg Paul from OMNI Brokerage; Tim Snodgrass; and Bill Winn. We were all actively involved.

We put an enormous amount of work into commercializing the Tenants in Common as a viable structure. Slowly, the tide turned in our favor. Triple Net, my law firm client at the time, was the biggest player, but the group was growing, along with my client base. Soon, I had twenty-four sponsor clients nationwide, and my law career was in high gear. My next stop was Southern California, when I became president of Triple Net.

Because everything was growing so rapidly, the industry leaders wanted to solidify our best practices and make sure that investors were treated fairly. We also needed to expand education and training for this complex, new investment program. So, a number of us industry insiders got together in Chicago, drafted bylaws, and officially formed a nonprofit known as the Tenant in Common Association (TICA), the original trade association for TICs and other alternative investments. I served two terms on the board, back in the day. We recently had a twenty-year reunion of our founding of TICA. (See Appendix K for a reunion photo of the old boy founders.)

As it became more established, the focus shifted to include more alternative investments and not just TICs. This included real estate funds and REITs, and even oil and gas–including all the people that sold alternative investments. So, the name changed once and then again when it became the Alternative & Direct Investment Securities Association (ADISA), which is still growing with a membership of approximately 5,000, as of this writing, with roughly 1,000 attendees at the last national conference in Las Vegas.

In 2002, the IRS essentially adopted our TIC structure in the form of a Revenue Procedure. This was odd because a "Rev. Proc.," as it is known, is used to inform taxpayers how to obtain an advance ruling from the IRS.

For a while, TICs worked really well, but their fatal flaw was the unanimous consent requirement for major decisions. Remember, the Delaware statutory trust's structure is different. With DSTs, you have a sponsor who runs the show. With the TIC structure, the investors were more actively involved. They had to approve major decisions and the sponsor's contract at least annually. And nothing against grannies in tennis shoes, but when these make up many of the investors, decisions are not always logical. Management of a property by a collection of amateur investors is vastly different from management by a professional real estate firm.

One of my industry colleagues once had a single-tenant mega deal—I mean, one of the biggest in our industry at the time, a very exciting single-tenant TIC investment out West. Something happened with the tenant that nobody could have anticipated, and he restructured the deal in a way that was magical. It was going to save everybody all their money over time. It was a perfect solution, but one TIC investor out of the group of owners wouldn't approve it. So, in the end, the loan went into default. The lender foreclosed, and everybody lost all their money because one investor didn't like the plan—one granny in tennis shoes caused a total loss for all investors.

I have a recollection of another colleague leading a long conference call on a TIC-owned office building in Philadelphia that had serious vacancy and limited funds on hand. At an hour and forty minutes, after reiterating the many reasons why he recommended using the available funds to pay for tenant improvements on new leases to increase cash flow, one of the investors asked, "So when am I getting my distributions?" She had not been listening and did not see the big picture, which was a choice: to improve the building for the ultimate benefit of all investors or to make a couple of distributions to investors until the funds ran out.

I also remember a little old TIC owner who loved drinking coffee in his Newport Beach TIC-owned shopping center. It was a beautiful shopping center near the beach with an emphasis on food that was owned by thirty-five TIC investors. In the TIC structure, all of the investors (meaning 100%) must approve a sale. When the time came to sell, he refused because his lifestyle revolved around that shopping center. Triple Net Properties, the sponsor, was offered an exorbitant price on several occasions, higher than anyone could've expected, but he refused. All the other investors approved, but he would not. Nothing anyone could say would change his mind. I talked to him until I was blue in the face, but he loved drinking coffee in "his shopping center." Later, the Great Financial Crisis of 2008 destroyed the value of that property, and it could not be sold for such a nice profit. Any wonder we don't use the TIC structure any longer?

This was before cell phones were common. Investors on a cruise and you need approval for something? How did you reach them? There were times when we sent representatives to their next port of call. Investor in the hospital? They still needed to sign the documents. Investor who has died? Well, that was a problem.

We don't have TIC calls anymore. I don't miss them.

The difference is that now, the DST sponsor makes the decisions to position the properties for financial success. It just makes sense. This is our expertise, so we focus on our investors-first strategies. In the DST structure, the sponsor makes these calls. The DST investors delegate authority to the sponsor to do the things that have to be done, the easy decisions and the hard ones. This is why lenders are more comfortable with a professional sponsor versus up to thirty-five amateurs in a TIC structure.

Beginning around 2008 with the economic decline associated with the Great Financial Crisis, TICs proved to be challenging and slowly fell out of favor. Many sponsors at that time were syndicating suburban office buildings using the TIC structure. When the economy blew up, it took many tenants down, big and small, and the office market was devastated. Many TIC properties were lost in foreclosure when the tenants abandoned their premises, leaving see-through buildings in their wake. This tainted the entire TIC structure.

Fortunately, back in 2004, the IRS had approved an alternative structure, the Delaware statutory trust, which does not have the issues that proved challenging with the TIC structure. Now, decades later, time has proven that the DST is a much better structure: confidentiality, liability protection, and non-recourse debt plus turn-key ownership with a professional sponsor making the decisions and operating the property. This evolution happened for a reason, and investors are all the better for it.

Like the maker of buggy whips when cars took the place of horses, I feel a bit of remorse over the years of sweat that went into commercializing the TIC structure, but I am happy for the thousands of exchangers who now have the benefit of a much better structure. That's progress. Onward with DSTs!

Chapter Twelve
DST Rules, Opportunities & Asset Classes

Essentials

Private real estate investments, such as DSTs, qualified opportunity zone funds, and development funds, are only sold to "accredited investors," who are deemed to have the sophistication and financial backing for such investments. The current accredited investor standard for a natural person is either $1 million net worth, excluding primary residence, or a minimum taxable income of $200,000 or $300,000 with spouse, in each of the two most recent years.

In Revenue Ruling 2004-86, the IRS ruled as follows:

1. The DST in the Ruling is an investment trust, under Section 301.7701-4(c) of the Treasury Regulations, which will be classified as a trust (and not a business entity) for federal tax purposes.

2. A taxpayer may exchange real property for an interest in the DST under Section 1031, provided the other requirements of Section 1031 are satisfied.

DST properties tend to be investment-grade, the highest quality of property with the highest caliber of tenants and managers. DSTs are offered in numerous asset classes, including:

- Housing:
  - Multifamily–Class A
  - Multifamily–Class B (value-add)
  - Multifamily–build for rent (BFR)
  - Multifamily–manufactured housing communities (MHCs)
- Medical facilities
- Corporate headquarters/Office facilities
- Industrial facilities
- Retail

Practice Tip for Realtors

Many tax-sensitive sellers want to know that there will be a desirable replacement property when they sell. Some may balk at signing a listing agreement with a realtor without solid replacement property options. The solution: introduce DSTs as a backup.

If the realtor is unable to procure a desirable whole replacement property, the seller can access a large pipeline of DST properties of all sizes, shapes, asset classes, and debt levels. The realtor gets a listing and first shot at sourcing the replacement property; the investor can rest assured that there will be a desirable replacement property when the time comes because the DST property will be there. A win-win!

Practice Tip for Investors with Cash

Here is a little-known fact. You have seen how DST interests are acquired by exchangers as replacement property in Section 1031 exchanges. But you can also buy them with cash, not a part of an exchange. Why would you do that? To get all the advantages of real estate ownership, including cash flow, appreciation, and tax benefits, including depreciation deductions. In fact, some investors will assemble a portfolio of DSTs as if they were building their own real estate mutual fund. With a small minimum investment ($50,000), it is easy for people to invest their cash in DSTs and to build a nice real estate portfolio and, unlike a REIT, the investor can pick and choose their properties.

Now, the icing on the cake will surprise you. With one exception, you cannot 1031 exchange an interest in a legal entity. You can't exchange partnership interests, stock, or trust interests–absolutely no way. But you can exchange DST interests. That is magical. So, you can invest cash in DSTs for the many benefits. When the DST's property appreciates and is sold, you structure the sale as an exchange under Section 1031 just as if you owned a whole property, and you can exchange over and over again. Now, you are on the road to a lifetime exchange program that, if held until death, will convert tax deferral under 1031 into tax forgiveness.

Welcome to swap till ya' drop in action. Who knew? Well, my team did, and now you do too.

Delaware statutory trusts are what Capital Square uses for our 1031 exchange programs.

It's a special kind of entity from a special kind of state. Delaware's small, and maybe you could say that they don't have much when it comes to size. But they certainly have entities. If you wanted to form a corporation, you could use Delaware. If you wanted to form a limited liability company, you could use Delaware. They have very good technology. You can go online and form an LLC in about a nanosecond. And the DST, the Delaware statutory trust, is–you guessed it–also formed in Delaware.

Back at the law firm, circa 2004, when we were forming hundreds of Delaware LLCs for exchange programs, my young kids asked me what I did for a living. They knew I was a lawyer but not the nitty gritty.

"I am an entity lawyer," I told them.

They responded, "What the heck is that?"

It is hard to explain, even today, but I hope you will appreciate the amount of time and effort we invested in the smallest detail, such as the form of legal entity, in creating exchange programs that qualify for exchange treatment along with the many benefits of DSTs and none of the deficiencies of TICs.

Delaware has been the state of choice for rating agencies and lenders going back to the early 2000s, when the now obsolete TIC structure was used for 1031 exchanges.

Why Delaware and not Virginia or New York?

Delaware has made a profitable business out of creating legal entities that are friendly to business owners and operators. This is a nice source of clean revenue from various fees that are charged to form and maintain entities. To create a profitable business, Delaware has established an expansive infrastructure to remotely form and maintain legal entities on a national basis; they have made a business out of this arcane service, and Delaware is the favored state in which to form legal entities for real estate.

In addition, Delaware has business-friendly laws and a reliable judicial system for disputes. It is not surprising then that the Treasury Department would choose Delaware as the state of choice in drafting the Revenue Ruling on 1031 exchanges.

A DST is a hybrid entity. It can be a lot of different things, so it is a chameleon. At Capital Square, we use DSTs in a thoughtful way to provide extra benefits beyond just qualifying for tax-deferral. Some of these we've discussed. Some of these we'll add into the conversation.

Starting off, if you invest in an industrial property DST and there's a horrible industrial accident, you're not liable. Your assets are protected. You might end up with an unfortunate investment, but you won't be personally liable. Your assets are protected. Like a stockholder in a corporation, you have no personal liability, and your assets are protected from claims of the DST's creditors and creditors of other investors.

DSTs are also an incredibly flexible entity and confidential. As noted, your name is not in the land records the way it would be if you were on the deed. If you were on the deed, people could look it up. They might call you for whatever reason, positive or negative. However, with a DST, your name won't appear anywhere in the land records.

The key to the DST is the Treasury Department–yes, the same people that gave us the qualified intermediaries so the Treasury lady's mom could exchange her rental house. The Treasury issued a Revenue Ruling, which is a statement of substantive law and binding on taxpayers. The Ruling concluded that a properly structured DST is like-kind real estate; a DST qualifies for 1031 treatment just like a whole property, just like a rental house, just like a parcel of land.

But let's compare the purchase of a typical "whole" property to a DST.

In the world of real estate, the mantra is *caveat emptor* or "let the buyer beware." The buyer must do their own due diligence investigation of a potential purchase or run the risk. Sure, there is a remedy when dealing with a fraudulent seller–for example, a seller who hides defects–but that is exceptionally rare. A real estate buyer must examine all aspects of the property before making a purchase. Many rely on realtors, lawyers, appraisers, inspectors, and the like to help with the due diligence, but there is no remedy for a buyer who fails to fully investigate a property and later discovers problems.

Compare *caveat emptor* to the world of DSTs. As we have discussed, DSTs are a security for securities laws purposes, where the standard is "full and fair disclosure." **The DST sponsor must make full and fair disclosure of all material facts, including risk factors, the business plan, financing, tenants, market information, economic data, the sponsor's background, etc. This is typically done in the Private Placement Memorandum (PPM) and is intended to provide a complete picture of the investment, both good and especially bad, so prospective investors can make an informed investment decision.**

In addition, DSTs are typically sold by securities broker-dealers who are licensed by the Financial Industry Regulatory Authority (FINRA). Under FINRA securities rules, broker-dealers must make an independent investigation of the sponsor and each DST offering before making a recommendation to a prospective investor. The broker-dealers must reach their own independent conclusion that the offering is fully and fairly disclosed, meets industry standards, and is suitable for the investor. Most broker-dealers engage independent due diligence firms, such as Mick & Associates or FactRight, to help them perform a thorough and independent investigation of the sponsor and each DST offering, including a site inspection.

In conclusion, in a typical whole property purchase, the buyer must do their own due diligence investigation, but in a DST offering, the sponsor provides a PPM containing all the material facts and associated documents. In addition, the regulators have created rules designed to protect investors and ensure that all the positive and especially negative factors have been fully and fairly disclosed to prospective investors. And in the securities world, there is a remedy–FINRA arbitration–for an investor who believes the broker-dealer violated the rules. So, take your pick: "let the buyer beware" or "full and fair disclosure."

You have the power to choose.

A DST program can also be used with any asset class. It could be multifamily, a medical office, a corporate headquarters, industrial, retail, you name it.

At Capital Square, we're mostly focused on housing. We have found that Class A and Class B apartments do very well in good times and bad. We've invested heavily in build-for-rent (BFR) communities made up of high-quality, professionally managed single-family homes for rent–providing residents with a unique living experience that blends the privacy of a single-family home with the convenience of multifamily management services. This includes leasing, landscaping, repairs, and maintenance. We've seen the demand skyrocket for BFR. We also have manu-factured housing communities (MHCs) in Florida that are age-re-stricted, which is a different concept. The MHC residents own their home. We own the land. We own the clubhouse. We own the pickleball courts. We've found that when residents move to well-run MHCs, they rarely leave. It's affordable, stable, and a very interesting way to invest. Plus, there's usually a waiting list to live at these properties.

At Capital Square, we're bullish on housing. When the pandemic hit, we were told to go home and work from home.

My first reaction was, "You're kidding me, right?"

Then my second reaction was, "Everyone needs housing." We discovered that our apartments were very stable. During the pandemic, we were collecting over 98% of our rents, higher than our projections, without any major complications. We were more stable than any previous time period. People didn't leave, and we found that there was a migration of people from the gateway cities, moving to the Southeast. Our properties are in the Southeast–Virginia through the Carolinas, Georgia, Florida, Texas, and Tennessee. Those housing markets were and still are doing very well.

We also like medical properties because nobody is getting any younger. Americans need more medical care every year, and doctors pay their rent. They're very good tenants. We like industrial as well, but we're incredibly picky about the tenants. The downside today is that the debt is much less favorable on medical and industrial properties compared to multifamily that has Fannie Mae and other government agency lenders charged with supporting housing.

At the time of the real estate recession in 2008, many exchange investors were overly concentrated in a single replacement property. They put a lot of money–sometimes all of their money– in one property. The Revenue Procedure limited TIC properties to thirty-five investors, maximum. Because the equity in a large TIC property was frequently more than $35 million, many sponsors imposed a $1 million minimum investment, so many investors put $1 million or more in a single property. Compare that to $50,000 per DST investment. A DST investor with that much in proceeds could invest in a large portfolio of DSTs.

When the real estate recession hit, it was ugly. I don't ever want to see that again. People lost their jobs, their homes, and decades of hard work. The moral of the story: don't put too many eggs in one basket. Diversify broadly. DSTs are great for this.

As another example of DSTs empowering investor lives, let me tell you about an engineer who lived out West. He planned on retiring soon and looked forward to travelling the world and enjoying time with his children and grandchildren, who had moved to the East.

In the 1980s, this engineer purchased a modest home for $100,000 on the GI Bill after leaving the military. He had rented the house for a long time. He was good with his hands and had invested sweat equity over the years in making substantial repairs and upgrades.

The house was in a desirable neighborhood as a rental, or it could be used as a "knock-down" for a new "McMansion." The house had a market value of approximately $600,000, the largest part of his personal net worth.

A year prior, our engineer had refinanced the house with a new first mortgage in the amount of $200,000. He enjoyed the rental income but became tired of the management hassles–tenants, toilets, and trash–and wanted to unburden himself from the property to be free to travel. With guidance from his financial advisor and CPA, he discovered that his return on investment was actually very low. He netted only $20,000 per year after expenses on his $600,000 asset.

He lived in a high-tax state and would have a very large tax bill to pay if he sold the house on a taxable basis. His tax basis was miniscule–just the original land value–because the house was fully depreciated. This engineer wanted out, but the taxes were too high. What was he to do?

Because of the punitive taxes, our engineer's financial advisor suggested a 1031 exchange. With help from advisors, he engaged a QI and signed the customary Exchange Agreement. At closing, the net proceeds of sale, less debt repayment, were wired to the QI and held in an exchange escrow account. Now, the 45/180 clock was running.

To qualify for 1031, this engineer was required to do two things:

- first, reinvest his net proceeds of $375,000 ($600,000–$200,000 debt repayment $25,000 closing costs) in real estate and

- second, have at least $200,000 of debt in place at closing.

In other words, he needed replacement property with a cost of $575,000 ($375,000 of equity + $200,000 of debt). He could use the cash proceeds of $375,000 for the downpayment plus closing and loan costs but must have at least $200,000 of replacement property debt.

This engineer had little experience with real estate acquisitions and loans; his last purchase was decades ago.

With the clock ticking, he contacted several real estate agents. One agent showed him rental houses, but if he wanted a rental house, he would have kept the nice one he had. He wanted a passive investment. Another realtor discussed a pipeline of net-leased retail properties across the nation, but most were too large for the amount he had to reinvest. Plus, the recent announcement of store closures, including blue-chip Walgreens, scared him. An internet realtor also showed him several dollar stores that might have worked, but our engineer did not like them with the report of recent bankruptcies in the papers.

With the clock continuing to tick, he was introduced to a financial advisor who specialized in DSTs. This financial advisor was a part of a Financial Industry Regulatory Authority (FINRA) licensed broker-dealer and had a large inventory of qualifying DST replacement properties. Working with the financial advisor, our engineer reviewed a number of desirable DST properties and elected to invest in three to diversify, following the financial advisor's guidance.

With only a week left on his forty-five-day identification deadline, this engineer from out West finalized his picks. The paperwork was prepared electronically; the closing documents were signed; and the QI funded the purchase price for each DST property.

All DSTs closed within forty-five days, and the cash started flowing from the new investments. DSTs are passive, and this engineer, who officially retired, was able to hit the road to travel and see his family. Victory!

Alternatively, if this engineer made his picks but did not close them by the forty-fifth day, it would have been no problem. On the forty-fifth day, he would have identified the DSTs of his choosing, thereby satisfying the forty-five-day deadline. Then, he could close on the DSTs at his leisure, easily satisfying the 180-day requirement. Whenever he closed on a given DST, the cash would start flowing on that property. Victory once again! We see the same result as the first scenario, just a little delayed.

With all this said, some taxpayers overlook a very basic fact: "identified" does not mean anything outside the 1031 setting. It does not mean the property is under contract, will pass due diligence, is a suitable candidate for a loan, and can be purchased. Therefore, as I've noted, it is imperative that the taxpayer has control over at least one of the identified replacement properties to be assured of completing the exchange. Many taxpayers include a DST property as a backup identification in case the other properties fall out, but again, Delaware statutory trusts have so many benefits, they may just be the best choice, no matter the other options.

We've worked with many investors over the years, and the beauty of these investments is that there are options. The investor gets to decide.

Even if the exchanger acquires a "whole" property, there may be funds left over. To avoid being taxed on the leftover funds—the "dribblings" as Buddy, my former law firm partner, used to say—the investor could also acquire a DST property in the precise amount of the excess funds. In this way, this investor would obtain 100% tax deferral.

DSTs are a hybrid, as I've said: they are real estate for Section 1031 tax purposes and also a security for securities laws purposes. DST programs are sponsored by reputable real estate firms known as "sponsors," who are in the business of creating Section 1031 replacement property programs. My firm, Capital Square, is one such sponsor. DSTs are sold as securities to investors in private placement offerings that are exempt from securities registration under SEC Regulation D. DSTs are sold through FINRA-licensed broker-dealers and registered investment advisors (RIAs) who subject sponsors to strict underwriting standards and due diligence.

All closing costs and reserves are included in the purchase price for a DST. The sponsor's fees and reimbursements are also included in the purchase price. There are a range of sponsor fees depending on the asset class and type of offering, including fees for acquisition, loan origination, asset and property management, and disposition. These fees vary from sponsor to sponsor. However, unlike a customary real estate closing, all of the up-front fees and costs are built into the purchase price. (See Appendix J for a sample DST closing statement.)

Typically, registered representatives of a broker-dealer sell DSTs with a commission that is built into the DST's offering price, while while Registered Investment Advisors (RIAs) typically charge either a consulting fee or make the DST an asset under management (AUM) on which a customary AUM fee is charged.

To invest in a DST, an individual must qualify as an "accredited investor," meaning that they have a $1 million net worth, excluding their primary residence, or a minimum taxable income of $200,000 or $300,000 with spouse. Legal entities have different standards.

The accredited investor requirement is imposed on DSTs to establish that the prospective investor has adequate financial resources and sophistication to understand the terms, including the risk factors outlined in the Private Placement Memorandum (PPM), the primary disclosure document for private offerings. As I've noted, it didn't have to be this way.

Back in 1991, when Triple Net was structuring the first of many TICs, we made a deliberate decision to limit TIC investments to accredited investors. We had an uphill battle on our hands educating the broker-dealers about a new tax structure and didn't want a fight about investor suitability, so we self-regulated by adopting the accredited investor standard. This became mandatory in the industry when TICA, the Tenant in Common Association, issued its first memorandum on best practices. I was a member of the drafting committee and a director at the time. (You already heard the details of the real estate investment industry's evolution and our efforts in shaping it in Chapter 11.) But, in short, the same standard is true on DSTs and qualified opportunity zone funds to this day. "Accredited investor" is the standard in the industry.

DSTs have a small minimum investment, typically $50,000. This means that even exchangers with smaller properties are able to acquire several DSTs to diversify and reduce their risk from investing in a single property. If an exchanger has a fairly modest amount of exchange proceeds, he or she can still acquire several DSTs to diversify and reduce the risk of investing in a single property.

As noted, most DST programs have debt in place because most exchangers need debt to qualify fully for Section 1031. The debt is non-recourse to the DST investors. The sponsor is responsible for any guarantees (typically, so called "bad boy carve-outs") associated with DST loans. There are also all cash (no debt) offerings for investors who do not want debt and high-leverage DST offerings for investors with higher debt on their relinquished property. A significant amount of time and effort goes into negotiating and closing the mortgage debt.

The financial advisors who sell DSTs insist on experienced and reputable real estate sponsors with the resources to close and operate the property for the holding period, typically up to ten years.

Each DST offering is required to have a due diligence report prepared by an independent due diligence firm. The reports are prepared for broker-dealers who have an obligation under FINRA rules to conduct independent due diligence. The due diligence firm examines the offering documents, due diligence documents, and loan documents and also makes a site inspection. All of the fees, costs, and reserves are considered before reaching a conclusion that the DST offering is properly represented in the PPM and meets industry standards.

When the DST purchases real estate, this is a full-blown real estate closing involving many parties:

- The DST as buyer
- The seller
- The seller's lawyers
- The lender
- The lender's lawyers
- A title and escrow company
- And often others

This results in the deed, mortgage, and other customary documents being recorded in the land records where the property is located. The DST is the purchaser on the land records, not the DST owners who are not disclosed in the land records.

By contrast, the purchase of DST interests is a snap. The sale is an internal transaction between the sponsor and the investor; it is not recorded in the land records. In addition, most sponsors provide an electronic drop box comprising all the real estate and due diligence documents, making for an efficient due diligence review and closing process. DST investors acquire a beneficial interest in the DST and an "Acknowledgment of Beneficial Ownership." (See Appendix I for a sample "Acknowledgment of Beneficial Ownership.")

DSTs typically pay their distributions monthly by direct deposit and issue quarterly reports on the property. Tax packages are sent annually, and the best sponsors provide annual property audits as well.

If any of this seems overwhelming, the beauty of the situation is that professionals live, breathe, eat, and sleep this stuff. We're obsessed with it and find it fascinating. Since the day Hunton & Williams asked me to step into that closet with that massive Lexus Nexus machine, my curiosity has been piqued about how investors can use real estate to build their family wealth over a lifetime. I built my entire company around this investors-first philosophy of legacy building.

DSTs have been designed to the advantage of taxpayers. There are opportunities out there to seize–opportunities many investors have never considered. My job–and my honor–is to help educate investors and to reveal the tremendous potential with tax-advantaged real estate investments.

Chapter Thirteen
Comparing Net Leases and Gross Leases*

The Essentials

Two basic types of leases are used for investment real estate: a net lease and a gross lease.

A "net lease" is a passive ownership structure frequently used for investment real estate. Net leases are commonly used in connection with retail properties, many industrial, and some office properties. With a net lease, the owner/landlord receives the rent net of specific expenses. That means the owner is not responsible for specified property expenses. Instead, the tenant is responsible for them. In a customary "triple net lease," the tenant is responsible for taxes, insurance, maintenance, and repairs in addition to rent. There are many variations, such as "absolute" and "double net," where the tenant bears more or less of the expenses.

A "gross lease" is an ownership structure where the owner/landlord is responsible for expenses. With a gross lease investment, such as an apartment community, the cost of expenses is essentially built into the rent paid by the tenants.

*Sections of this chapter are adapted from an article published in The DI Wire in May 2023.

Further Details

Net leases are commonly used for single-tenant properties. With only one tenant, the property is either 100% occupied or 100% vacant. This means that if the single tenant fails, the investment is likely to fail. Understanding the risk profile of different lease structures is essential for smart investing.

Gross leases are most common with multifamily properties. The cost of property expenses is essentially built into the rent paid on an apartment lease, and because most apartment leases are of short duration, the owner is usually able to raise the rent to cover increases in operating expenses. At any given time, new tenants are coming to the apartment community, and old tenants are leaving. During good times, the rent goes up. During bad times, the landlord can reduce the rent and has several levers to pull to retain occupancy.

The attributes of net leases versus gross leases have a profound impact on the selection of investment programs. A wise man once said, "a net lease is the greatest ownership structure for real estate investments...until...it isn't."

Personally, I love net leases, but I also hate them. When they go bad, I can't fix them; no one can.

Let's analyze a real-world example of a customary Delaware statutory trust program for exchangers. Based on my personal experiences, there tends to be a dividing line between investors who need to live on distributions from the investment and those who have less need for immediate cash flow, prioritizing growth of income and capital appreciation.

There is a tendency to invest in net-leased programs for investors who have greater need for immediate cash flow. Alternatively, many wealthier investors favor multifamily programs with gross leases because they prioritize capital appreciation over initial cash flow. This is not to critique different types of investors but to demonstrate that the attributes of net versus gross leases have a real, tangible bearing on investment programs in the real world. It is a testament to the DST industry that sponsors can tailor different investment programs, and financial advisors are able to select programs that meet the needs of different types of investors.

In a net lease, the tenant typically manages their own real estate and operates within the premises. Because of this, there is very little for the owner/landlord to do, making net leases a desirable passive ownership structure. This can be very good for the owner, but it also can be very bad, depending on the circumstances. Net leases usually operate perfectly well; in good times, the absence of management hassles is a benefit. But in bad times, there is very little the owner can do to correct the situation.

What happens in good and bad times with net-leased real estate? Let's use the classic, single-tenant net lease as an illustration. An investment-grade tenant, Walgreens, for example, leases 100% of the property for use as a pharmacy. In good times, the owner receives the rent and reimbursements as set forth in the lease, no more and no less. (Spoiler alert: in an apartment lease, the owner usually does better in good and bad times.)

In the case of bad news, the name-brand pharmacy "goes dark" by closing the store. The tenant is still obligated under the lease and continues to pay the rent, but "going dark" can have seriously negative ramifications for the owner. This can trigger a cash flow sweep by the owner's lender, depriving the owner of cash flow. It can also result in cancellation of necessary property and casualty insurance. And, finally, this is likely to result in serious erosion of value on a future sale. All of this is completely outside the owner's control. What can the owner do? Not much. Going dark is not prohibited in many retail leases, which means the owner has no recourse against the tenant.

Lease terms vary depending on property type and region. In some cases, going dark may violate the lease. If so, the owner may be able to terminate the lease and regain possession. But terminating the lease may result in loss of the rent and, as a practical matter, many tenants who have gone dark will be unable to pay the rent. In the pharmacy example, this creditworthy tenant has substantial resources to continue paying the rent, but the same is not true with less established tenants.

Keep in mind that most owners need the rent to pay their debt service.

Also, in terminating the net lease, the owner will become obligated to pay taxes, insurance, maintenance, and repair costs that were the tenant's obligation under the lease. Thus, by terminating the lease, the owner may have no rent from the tenant and, at the same time, may have to pay debt services, taxes, insurance, maintenance, and repair costs, all out of pocket. Unless the owner has substantial cash on hand, loss of the property to the lender in foreclosure may become a real possibility following a lease termination.

So, when it comes to investing in a net lease, to quote a famous movie cop, "Are you feeling lucky?"

Conversely, what happens in good and bad times with a gross lease of an apartment community? Let's say you own a 300-unit apartment community. The owner/landlord is responsible for all expenses, hence the term "gross lease." The cost of expenses is essentially built into the rent paid on an apartment lease, and because most apartment leases are in short duration, the owner typically can raise the rent to cover increases in operating expenses. History has proven that apartment investments meet or exceed the rate of inflation.[vii]

Unlike a passive net lease, apartment leases are very active. The owner can either self-manage or hire a third-party property manager. At any given time, new tenants are coming to the apartment community, and old tenants are leaving. During good times, the rent goes up. During bad times, the landlord has several levers to pull. To maintain occupancy with this rolling tenant base, the landlord has the ability to cut the rent, offer concessions, or provide gift cards and the like. Through exceptional management and expertise, the owner can improve their position in spite of challenging economic times.

By contrast, the owner of a net-leased property typically is stuck and can't do very much to improve their situation short of finding a new tenant and, even then, usually at substantial out-of-pocket expense for leasing commissions and tenant improvement costs plus downtime and free rent. During the Great Financial Crisis of 2008, most apartment communities functioned reasonably well; rents were adjusted downward when needed to retain occupancy, and there were very few foreclosures. This was not the case with many net-leased properties, especially office properties that were wiped out along with their owners.

A net lease has a fixed term of years and typically optional extensions that the tenant may exercise to extend the term of the lease. The option to extend is exercised–or not–by the tenant. The landlord/owner cannot count on optional extensions being exercised. At the end of the lease term, the landlord/owner has no assurance that the tenant will renew. If the tenant does not renew, the property will be vacant, and the rent will stop. No rent may be received for a substantial period of downtime. Also, the landlord may be on the hook to pay a leasing commission and tenant improvement costs, and the replacement tenant may insist on a period of free rent.

Thus, as the lease melts down, so may the value of the property. It has been said by a famous due diligence officer, Bryan Mick, that a net lease is like an ice cube: "As the years pass toward expiration, a net lease melts down and has the potential to lose value."[viii]

If all that were not bad enough, a buyer is highly unlikely to pay full price for a net-leased property with a short remaining lease term. The situation can become even more dire upon approaching the repayment date on the owner's loan, when a sale or refinance will be necessary to repay the debt. Failure to refinance or sell may result in loss of the property to the lender.

Compare this to an apartment lease. Apartment leases are typically short term, commonly one year. This means that every year, many leases will be renewed, and many leases will be replaced with new tenants. Apartment communities are not 100% occupied or 100% vacant; they remain mostly occupied and roll through with new tenants as a part of the business plan. They bring full value on sale with a rolling rent roll. Compare this to a net-leased investment with a short lease maturity that is unlikely to bring full price.

What about rent increases? Many net leases have fixed rent increases–so-called, "rent bumps." It is typical to have either annual increases or increases over time. For example, 2% per year or 10% every five years. This tends to be satisfactory except in periods of rapid inflation. In an apartment lease, the rent can be reset to market on a regular basis since apartment leases are of short duration. Thus, in periods of rapid inflation, apartment rents go up rapidly while net lease rent increases are fixed.

Take the period of hyper-inflation in the early 2020s. How would the owner feel about a net lease with 10% rent increases every five years? With high inflation, an apartment lease would be preferred over a net lease that may lose value.

In a multi-tenant investment, the owner/landlord has a cushion via the rent and reimbursements from numerous tenants. The same is true in multifamily properties, where there are a large number of tenants (300 tenants, for example) to provide a big cushion. This makes multifamily and multi-tenant properties less risky from a tenant standpoint because of the larger number of tenants paying rent and reimbursements.

Again, to quote our movie cop, "Are you feeling lucky?" with a property that is either 100% occupied or 100% vacant?

It should go without saying: *caveat emptor,* let the buyer beware. It's a familiar phrase to be sure. Circumstances will differ, and investors should seek the guidance of qualified real estate and financial professionals before making an investment.

Because the burden is on the purchaser in a real estate transaction, extensive due diligence is critical to avoiding serious problems. The due diligence can be very extensive, involving a title search, environmental study, survey, property condition report, roof report, study of the rent roll, review of leases and correspondence, and more. Frequently, the zoning should be investigated, and an appraisal needs to be obtained for a lender. This is a mammoth task for an exchanger purchasing a whole property.

Many exchangers are regular folks who lack the skill and experience to oversee the due diligence process. That is why many hire real estate professionals to assist with the due diligence, commonly a lawyer and realtor. Lawyers typically charge by the hour, and the cost can get out of hand if the property has issues. Plus, the due diligence process can take a substantial amount of time. Don't forget, the Section 1031 clock is tick tick ticking away.

On the other hand, in a DST, the sponsor will take care of all due diligence and provide the studies and reports in an electronic drop box that the investor and advisors can access at any time. That is one of the many benefits of DSTs: the due diligence is completed by an experienced real estate team; the property has already been acquired by the DST's sponsor; and the loan is in place if the DST is leveraged. All of that takes the stress out of the due diligence process. Acquiring a DST replacement process is a breeze. Just ask a DST investor.

Chapter Fourteen

Tax-Advantaged Investments through Qualified Opportunity Zones

Essentials

Qualified opportunity zone (QOZ) funds were created to stimulate long-term private investments in low-income urban and rural communities by providing tax deferral and exclusion on the sale of any capital asset. Conceived as part of the Tax Cuts and Jobs Act of 2017, QOZ funds are intended to promote impact-creating developments in distressed areas by providing tax benefits to investors. This bipartisan legislation was sponsored by Senator Tim Scott (R-SC) and Senator Cory Booker (D-NJ). Most QOZ funds will build a new building, for example, a new apartment community, in a qualified opportunity zone.

With two levels of tax advantages, investing in QOZ funds can lead to permanent elimination of capital gains taxes. The initial benefit defers capital gains taxes from the initial sale of stocks, bonds, real estate, businesses, and other assets. By investing in a QOZ, those taxes are deferred until the taxpayer's 2026 tax return (typically, due by April 15, 2027 for an individual taxpayer). The second benefit is tax forgiveness. Gains on the sale of the fund's building will be forgiven if the investment is held for at least ten years.

QOZ funds typically develop real estate projects in designated opportunity zones. By combining investor capital and a construction loan, QOZ funds are constructing new buildings across the nation, including much-needed housing.

Practice Tip

Invest capital gains from any sale into a QOZ fund within 180 days of the sale. Unlike Section 1031 exchanges, these capital gains may have resulted from the sale of any asset, including:

- Stocks
- Bonds
- Mutual funds
- Real estate, including a failed exchange
- Business sale
- Other capital assets
- Art
- Cryptocurrency

A growing number are investing in QOZ funds to build family wealth with the goal of tax forgiveness when the ten-year holding requirement has been satisfied.

B y this point, you know Capital Square as a national real estate firm focused on tax-advantaged real estate investments, including replacement property for Section 1031 exchanges using the DST structure. We're also well known for the firm's development team, building mixed-use, Class A multifamily communities in the Southeast. We've had six projects in Richmond, Virginia, including CoStar's 2024 multifamily building of the year, the Otis, not to mention our developments in Raleigh, North Carolina; Charleston, South Carolina; and Knoxville, Tennessee. These are all in qualified opportunity zones, with a QOZ fund sponsored by Capital Square. We're talking nearly a billion dollars in value and over 2,000 new apartment units. This is another tax-advantaged real estate opportunity we need to discuss.

The other day, I was speaking about our Knoxville QOZ fund, and for the occasion, I was dressed informally. Knoxville is home to the University of Tennessee, so I wore their orange jersey to commemorate this QOZ fund. Welcome to the zone, the opportunity zone. Welcome to the Land of OZ for tax deferral and exclusion.

QOZ legislation was part of the Tax Cuts and Jobs Act of 2017. That seems like a long time ago. We've all been through so much since then. But when it was created, the goal was to generate economic activity in certain economically distressed and rural areas through private investment. The legislation provides both tax deferral and exclusion for investors, and we'll talk about that. However, you might wonder how the zones were determined, so let's start there.

The governor of each state could designate up to 25% of eligible census tracts as opportunity zones, and now there are nearly 9,000 active opportunity zones across the country.

Capital Square's QOZ projects create economic revitalization throughout the Southeast, while assisting investors with tax deferral and exclusion strategies and favorable returns. Much like Section 1031 exchanges through Delaware statutory trusts, the goal is to reinvest capital gains for elimination of taxes. But QOZ funds go further than 1031, which focuses exclusively on like-kind real estate exchanges. Capital gains from the sale of any asset can be invested in QOZ funds to achieve tax deferral and exclusion. That is exceptionally broad and one of the best tax advantages in the entire Tax Code.

Capital gains may have resulted from the sale of stocks, bonds, mutual funds, a business, art, cryptocurrency, or other assets–yes, including real estate. By investing in a QOZ, the taxpayer can defer their capital gains taxes, and they're deferred until their 2026 tax return (due on April 15, 2027 for individual taxpayers). **If the QOZ investment is held for ten years, the gain will be excluded when the fund's building is sold. I'm talking total tax forgiveness. No swapping, dropping, or death of the investor is necessary. This is why QOZ funds have become so popular recently.**

When the time comes to sell real estate, many owners will consider a Section 1031 exchange, but some will want to consider a QOZ investment. This is also the only viable option on a blown exchange–if the taxpayer didn't structure the sale as an exchange upfront (with an Exchange Agreement and a QI) or if they tried to exchange but failed. The good news is that you may still defer and exclude the gain by making a QOZ investment. And remember the hated depreciation recapture in the discussion of Section 1031– that painful tax at 25%? Well, by making a QOZ investment on the sale of real estate, that tax is also deferred and ultimately excluded along with the federal capital gains tax.

Let's take a minute and compare QOZ funds to Section 1031 exchanges, which are much more common and have been around since 1921. Section 1031 is a golden oldie. It's definitely my favorite as a tax lawyer, if you couldn't tell. As you know, these exchanges are the primary tax strategy for the real estate industry. Again, approximately 20–25% of all commercial real estate transactions are likely structured as 1031 exchanges.

Now, Section 1031 defers taxes, both federal and state, from the sale of investment or business real estate. This is very important to real estate investors but strictly limited to investment or business real estate. We're talking about real estate held for appreciation or income, or used in a business, not your principal residence, a second home, or real estate abroad, and definitely not any other asset–just real estate. Section 1031 is my specialty as a tax lawyer, but it is very strict in terms of the rules and the timing, as we've discussed.

QOZ funds are much broader. You can defer and exclude capital gains taxes, federal and most states, from the sale of any asset. This bears repeating, any asset–not just real estate but any asset, including stocks, bonds, Bitcoin, businesses, and so much more. Some may use opportunity zones as a backup for a failed 1031 exchange. That's one of two reasons QOZs are included in this discussion of tax-advantaged real estate. The second is that I love this stuff, and the more everyone knows about tax-advantaged real estate investment, the more everyone can work toward building their own family's legacy.

QOZ funds have no Exchange Agreement, no qualified intermediary, and no debt replacement requirement. Plus, the time to reinvest is favorable. You have 180 days to reinvest the gain. It works really well: just make an election on your tax return for the year of sale. Very simple.

If the taxpayer is a tax partnership, there's a special rule. You can go to the end of the tax year, typically December 31st, and the partnership can elect to make a QOZ investment; if not, then each of the partners, individually, can make their own election to invest their share of the gain in a QOZ. That means December 31st, plus 180 days for each of the partners. **This permits partners to separate. Some can make QOZ investments, and others can cash out.** This is another interesting comparison with Section 1031 exchanges. It is very difficult to cash out partners in an exchange. The "drop and swap" structure used to liquidate partners in an exchange will test the patience of investors and their wallets with big legal fees. But you don't have that with partnerships and QOZs, where each partner can go their separate way, and they have an extra 180 days from the tax year end.

I have to add that not all states conform to federal law. Most do, but California and New York do not conform to federal law on opportunity zones. Only the federal tax benefits exist in those states. It's important to note also that in a Section 1031 exchange, using the Delaware statutory trust (DST) structure, we're talking about a turn-key investment where the property is acquired by the sponsor in advance. The debt is in place, if the DST has leverage. The property is leased up. It is a done deal, and it generates stable cash flow with very few surprises. QOZ funds are different. They are development projects. The building has to be planned, built, leased up, and permanently financed for a ten-year hold. There's greater risk in development and a greater reward with the tax benefits and returns from cash flow and appreciation. QOZs typically have much higher returns, but the cash flow only starts once the property is fully stabilized. The icing on the cake: in ten years, the QOZ's building can be sold, and the taxes will be forgiven. And you don't have to die to obtain tax forgiveness.

In a DST, tax rules require the sale of the property when the loan matures. That's typically ten years, at which point the investors will likely structure another 1031 exchange, the series of exchanges where they swap till they drop. It's a great tax strategy, tax forgiveness on death, but you have to die to get it.

In the land of OZ, you have tax forgiveness at the end of the ten-year holding period. The investor doesn't have to die to get it. That's a little better, right? More than a little.

Let's talk about designated QOZs versus "blind pools." QOZ funds are sponsored by reputable real estate firms like Capital Square, firms that have passed muster with broker-dealers and third-party due diligence firms. The QOZ securities are typically sold by licensed broker-dealers or registered investment advisors, and there are two types of funds. Many of the larger firms raise a billion or two in what's called a blind pool. You don't know exactly what you're getting. You do know the parameters. You know how much they're raising. You know the sponsor plans to develop buildings, and they are intended to qualify as a QOZ. But that's it. Capital Square has a different approach.

At Capital Square, each QOZ fund is a single property: one fund, one property, one QOZ. The property and all the details are fully identified, disclosed with a business plan and a pro forma all set forth in great detail in the offering documents. We encourage financial advisors and investors to tour the site and to meet the development team. We believe this helps investors with an important investment choice by kicking the tires and reaching an informed decision about the opportunity.

Are QOZs satisfying the government's stated purpose of creating economic opportunity? I'm here to tell you an emphatic, "yes!"

According to FTI Consulting, a market-leading global consulting firm, Capital Square's QOZs have had a positive impact on the economies of the neighborhood, city, and state where each property is located. Data published in early 2025 revealed that the combined annual construction impacts for Capital Square's projects in Virginia, North Carolina, Tennessee, and South Carolina include approximately 2,010 jobs supported during the construction phase, as well as $197 million in GDP, and $41 million in total tax revenues. Projected combined operations impacts include approximately 345 ongoing jobs supported annually, $81 million in GDP annually, and $17 million in total tax revenues annually.[ix] These revenues help support other public investments, such as education, highways, and public safety.

Bottom line, QOZs create jobs and positive economic impact. We are satisfying the legislative mission by creating jobs and economic opportunities across the Southeast, and even more work can be done in these areas.

In conclusion, QOZ funds provide arguably the greatest tax benefit in the entire Tax Code. I don't have the Code on my desk, but sometimes I do think about that golf cart to carry it all. Now, forgiveness of taxable gain after a ten-year holding period is exceptional. The pool of investors for QOZ funds is massive. For anyone who has a capital gain, not just real estate as applies in Section 1031, the logistics are simple. Elect QOZ status on your tax return and invest the gain in a QOZ fund within 180 days. Then you're along for the ride. What does the ride look like?

We have a QOZ sponsor who buys a land parcel in a qualified opportunity zone. That's the starting point, locating the lot suitable for a new development in a qualified opportunity zone. The sponsor usually builds a building with capital from the QOZ investors and a construction loan. When the construction is complete, the sponsor leases up the building to the point of stabilization. That's typically around 90% occupancy. Then the sponsor permanently finances the building. This generates excess loan proceeds after repaying the construction loan.

This is exactly what Capital Square has done repeatedly. Here is the cadence:

- Capital Square purchases lots in a qualified opportunity zone. The lots are ideally suited for planned developments.
- Then, we develop buildings with capital from investors and a construction loan.
- We lease up the buildings and, upon stabilization, permanently finance them.
- This increased value from stabilization results in excess loan proceeds, so we make a special distribution to the investors, which is tax free.

We've done this many, many times–every time so far. When the proceeds are in excess of the construction loan, there are excess proceeds. It's a special distribution without taxation, and that's worth repeating: there is no tax on this special distribution to investors.

This is the cash distributed to investors to pay their taxes due with their 2026 tax returns (typically due by April 15, 2027 for individuals). We've delivered the funds to investors to pay their taxes years in advance of their tax due date. Finally, the icing on the cake: after a ten-year holding period, the buildings can be sold, and the taxable gain that otherwise would be triggered is forgiven. And, unlike 1031, you don't have to die to get tax forgiveness.

Welcome to the Land of OZ, the land of tax deferral and exclusion of taxation from the sale of any asset.

Chapter Fifteen
Tax-Advantaged Investments through Real Estate Investment Trusts (REITs)

Essentials

Approximately 145 million American households invest in real estate investment trusts (REITs) directly or indirectly, via their IRAs, 401(k)s, and pension plans.[x] REITs own a whopping $3.5 trillion in assets across the nation.[xi] They invest in a wide range of real estate asset classes and property types, including housing, medical, office, and retail properties.

REITs pay their stockholders a dividend that comes from the net income generated by the real estate. REITs are required to distribute 90% of their taxable income to stockholders, which makes them an excellent choice for income-oriented investors.

Why invest in REITs?

1. Total return
2. Low correlation to traded stocks
3. A hard asset
4. Investment-grade real estate
5. Professional management

Real estate investment trusts typically come in three varieties:

1. Equity REITs, which own properties to generate income
2. Mortgage REITs, which make loans to property owners
3. Hybrid REITs, which invest in both properties and loans

The discussion below will focus on equity REITs that own real estate to generate income for stockholders.

Capital Square is a special kind of investment manager. Specializing in tax-advantaged real estate investments, we're well known for our Delaware statutory trust investments for 1031 exchange investors who own real estate and want tax deferral. We're also well known for our qualified opportunity zone fund investments for taxpayers who have any sort of capital gain and want to defer and exclude the taxes. Recently, we've sponsored development funds, which raise capital from investors to develop new buildings for higher returns in a shorter holding period. Another of my personal favorites is Capital Square Housing Trust, our real estate investment trust (REIT) that acquires and manages apartment communities and other housing assets in growth markets throughout the Southeast. Our aim with the REIT is to own a portfolio of housing properties that generates a combination of stable income, capital appreciation, and a hedge against inflation for our investors.

As you might have guessed by this point, I have always been bullish on education. I frequently make educational presentations on Section 1031, qualified opportunity zones, REITs, depreciation, cost segregation/bonus depreciation, etc. It's been at least thirty-five years since I started speaking on tax-advantaged real estate, presenting to realtors, lawyers, CPAs, broker-dealers, and regular folks. Many of the "shaggy dog" stories described in this book come from the dark recesses of my brain, in a stream of consciousness while presenting on one of these topics.

Education is critically important, as we help investors and advisors "swap till they drop." Maybe it's a corny expression, but that's how it works. And there's so much more to the tax-advantaged real estate investment conversation. We've covered qualified opportunity zones. Now, let's turn to real estate investment trusts.

So, you ask, what is a REIT?

A real estate investment trust (REIT) is a corporation that owns, operates, or finances income-producing real estate. Millions of Americans invest in REITs for stable income growth, capital appreciation, and inflation protection.[xii]

REITs provide an investment opportunity like a mutual fund that makes it possible for everyday Americans, not just the wealthy, not just Wall Street, not just big investment banks and hedge funds, but everyday Americans to enjoy the many benefits of real estate investments. Investing in a REIT makes you a stockholder. Stockholders share in REIT earnings via dividends without having to participate in the real estate business. That means you can invest in REIT stock and enjoy the benefits of real estate ownership without having to become a real estate professional–without having to buy, manage, or operate real estate.

REITs are an ideal investment for everyday folks, and dividends are key. REITs are designed to generate stable dividends, and those dividends tend to increase over time with the potential for capital appreciation and inflation protection.

Real estate investment trusts have a long history, and that history shows that REITs have delivered a strong total return.[xiii] You hear that term over and over again: "total return." What's a total return? Well, it's dividends, and in the case of a REIT, they are historically stable and increase over time, along with the potential for appreciation in the stock value that generates a profit on sale.

Congress created REITs back in 1960. In short, equity REITs pool the capital of many investors to own and operate real estate. You'll hear that theme frequently, whether it is the fractional ownership model of Delaware statutory trusts or qualified opportunity zone funds, where investors pool capital focused on a single property, or numerous investors pooling their capital to invest in a portfolio of properties, as in a REIT. In each of these scenarios, investors have the opportunity to invest in properties they couldn't afford to own individually. The goal is to make high-quality, income-producing real estate accessible and available to regular folks, average citizens.

Historically, the best real estate, what we call "investment-grade real estate," was mostly owned by wealthy individuals, institutions, investment banks, and funds. Think of this as the rich and powerful. The little folks couldn't afford to own investment-grade real estate, but REITs democratize the ownership of real estate. REITs allow regular folks to invest in a diversified portfolio with professional management, and that's a big deal.

We'll talk about professional management, but first, think about how many investors can afford to buy a $100 million building. Not very many. How many can afford to buy a portfolio of $100 million buildings worth billions? Hardly any. But REITs allow anyone to participate. REITs have democratized the ownership of real estate, so anyone can own a piece of the rock, so to speak, through the purchase of REIT stock.

We have talked about REIT dividends that historically have grown over time and capital appreciation. In addition, history has shown that real estate provides inflation protection, especially to multifamily housing assets, such as those acquired by Capital Square Housing Trust, my firm's REIT. Dr. Peter Linneman, Capital Square's economic advisor, is a world-famous economist who specializes in real estate. He taught at the Wharton School for a long time and studied under four or five Nobel Prize winners. He has the rare ability to explain complex economic data in understandable terms that are useful in real world investing. In his white paper called "The Golden Age of Multifamily Investing," prepared for Capital Square, Dr. Linneman explains that multifamily leases are typically short term (one year), which means that rents can be adjusted periodically. Also, multifamily rents typically increase over time, and because of that increase, history shows that they meet or exceed the rate of inflation. His research examines the last fifty years, during which time rents have typically exceeded the rate of inflation.[xiv] That is a comfort to many retirees who rely on REIT dividends to supplement their income in retirement.

We also talk about total return, that is dividends plus growth with inflation protection. REITs pay most of their earnings in dividends. They're an excellent source of income for cash investors and also for so-called qualified funds—those are your retirement accounts—in part because there's no "unrelated business taxable income" (UBTI) when qualified funds are invested in REITs. Note: UBTI is a tax on otherwise tax-free retirement accounts (qualified funds) that violate certain fundamental rules, for example, use of debt to increase returns. Congress did not want tax-free investors, who already have an advantage from their tax status, to compete unfairly with taxable investors.

Many financial planners use REITs in retirement to provide stable income with capital appreciation and inflation protection. REITs allow anyone to invest in portfolios of assets the same way they would invest in other industries, through the purchase of stock. REIT stockholders earn a share of the REIT's income, a dividend, without having to buy, manage, or finance real estate.

Approximately 150 million American households invest in REITs, and they do that either directly or through their retirement accounts. That's a lot of people. It's a lot of households. REITs are an enormously important industry in our country. They own approximately 575,000 properties.[xv] They invest in a wide range of real estate assets. There are multifamily REITs, like Capital Square Housing Trust, along with REITs that specialize in offices, warehouses, retail properties, medical facilities, and even hotels.

Some REITs have a geographic orientation. For example, Capital Square Housing Trust primarily invests in the Southeast: Virginia, the Carolinas, Georgia, Florida, Texas, and Tennessee.

How do most REITs make money? It's very simple. REITs lease space and collect rents. Most rents increase over time, providing rent growth. This rent growth protects earnings by offsetting the impact of inflation, which is another potential benefit from investing in REITs: inflation protection.

REIT income is paid out to stockholders by way of dividends, and the tax rules require that at least 90% of a REIT's taxable income must be paid out in dividends. That's why REITs are an excellent income generator. They are required to pay most of their earnings in dividends. Many investors use REIT investments to supplement their income in retirement.

Compare REITS to a growth investment like a startup venture. Specifically, startups typically do not have any cash flow to make distributions to investors. REITs are at the opposite end of the spectrum. REITs typically invest in cash-flowing real estate and pay out most of their earnings in dividends. That's why they're such a great income-generating vehicle.

Why invest in REITs? Five reasons: total return, low correlation to traded stocks, a hard asset, investment-grade real estate, and professional management:

- **One:** Historically, REITs have delivered competitive total returns over time.[xvi] That means steady dividends that increase over time with long-term capital appreciation (plus inflation protection).

- **Two:** REITs have a low correlation to traded stocks. This is a little more complicated a notion, but it makes REITs an excellent portfolio diversifier. Let's say you own all of your assets in traded stocks, and the market crashes. All of your assets are likely to crash. But by investing a portion of your portfolio in REITs that are not correlated to the stock market, they wouldn't go down just because the stock market went down. You would be diversified. By adding REITs to a stock portfolio, investors can reduce their overall portfolio risk and increase total returns. That's what the history shows. You can go to NAREIT, the REIT trade association, and they have a load of statistics showing that REITs reduce overall portfolio risk and also increase returns, at the same time.[xvii] This is similar to our discussion of diversification with DSTs. **By diversifying your investment portfolio with REITs, you are reducing the risk and increasing returns. It's a double benefit.** What's not to like about that? To quote a famous British guitar player, "That ain't working. Money for nothing." Anyone remember MTV?

- **Three:** REITs invest in hard assets, for example housing assets, such as apartment communities. People need places to live. Housing is a necessity.

- **Four:** REITs typically invest in investment-grade real estate, the best assets in the nation, too large and too expensive for an individual investor to acquire on their own.

- **Five:** REITs have the best real estate managers in the nation. Their goal is to maximize shareholder value by positioning their properties to attract tenants and increase the net operating income (increase rents and reduce expenses) to increase dividends.

There you go: five reasons to invest in REITs. Why wait?

Now, who invests in REITs? That's easy. Everyone, regular folks, directly through the purchase of stock, or indirectly through their pension plans, mutual funds, or exchange-traded funds, along with endowments, foundations, family offices, and insurance companies.

There are many types of REITs, but most are equity REITs. They own or operate income-producing property. There are also mortgage REITs that provide financing for real estate, and then you have public, non-traded REITs. Those are registered as a public company with the Securities Exchange Commission (SEC), but they don't trade on a stock exchange. Finally, you have private REITs, which are private companies that qualify for REIT status and are exempt from registration with the SEC.

How you qualify as a REIT is a somewhat complicated story. The rules are strict. REITs invest in real estate, and they must pay out 90% of their taxable income to stockholders, as I've noted. Those are the first two requirements. They're managed by a board of directors, typically with a majority of independent directors, and they're widely held. The last two requirements dictate a minimum of one hundred stockholders and a prohibition on having too close of a relationship among stockholders. No five or fewer stock-holders can own 50% or more of a REIT.

So, REITS invest in real estate, pay out most of their income in dividends, and are widely held. They're managed by a board of directors, the majority of whom are independent. These rules are designed to protect the interests of stockholders.

What type of properties do REITs own and manage? Multifamily or residential properties are typical, but also medical facilities, shopping centers, retail properties, warehouses, office buildings, and industrial properties. Some REITs specialize. For example, Capital Square Housing Trust invests in housing assets, and other REITs invest in multiple asset classes.

Regarding tax issues and REITs, there are two big ones. The first is that there's no unrelated business taxable income (UBTI) for qualified funds (tax-exempt retirement accounts) that invest in REITs, as I've noted. That's an important point worth repeating. In short, when you're investing your retirement funds, you don't have to worry about the UBTI tax. REITs are exempt.

Also, corporations typically generate two levels of tax, a tax at the corporate level, 21% as of this writing, and also at the share-holder level, 37% at the top rate. Add those two up, and you have a lot of taxes, but not a REIT.

REIT earnings are typically subject to a single level of tax at the stockholder level. You remember, REITs have to pay out 90% of their taxable income in dividends. Since most earnings are distributed to stockholders, REITs generally do not pay corporate income tax. So, we get to one level of tax, and then on certain categories of income, there's no tax. This one's my favorite. There are no taxes on distributions that represent a return of capital. So, in conclusion, REITs generate one level of tax at the stock-holder level generally and no tax on return of capital distributions. And if you're investing retirement funds, your qualified funds, there's no unrelated business taxable income. So, that is all good.

Now, let's talk about the impact of taxes. Imagine a housing-fo-cused REIT has a $9 per share price. It has a dividend of 5.61%, and then there's the impact of taxes. Consider the highest federal rate of 37% and the tax on net investment income of 3.8%. Then consider your state tax that varies. At present, Virginia is presently a mere 5.75%, while California is 10.30%.

You add up all those taxes, and you end up between 46% and 51%. But because of the REIT structure with the benefit of depreciation and other deductions, the dividend is currently fully sheltered. That means, no federal or state income tax on the dividends as of Q1 2025. The after-tax equivalent return is anywhere from 10.5% to 11.47%, depending on your state's tax rate. This means you would have to make between 10.5% to 11.47% on a taxable basis in some other investment to have the equivalent of this 5.61% dividend. That's no tax on the 5.61%, federal or state, and that is the equivalent of 10.5% to 11.47%.

Again, it may sound complicated, but the simple version is that REIT tax benefits produce greater after-tax returns.

Lastly, let's talk about the tax matrix. Real estate is tax favored. We've discussed Section 1031 exchanges in detail, for when you're selling investment real estate. We've also talked about the benefit of qualified opportunity zone funds to defer and exclude taxes. When it comes to your cash just sitting around, the REIT is an excellent, diversified real estate investment designed to generate stable income and growth with inflation protection. It has tax benefits. REITs can be a way to reimagine and reinvigorate your qualified funds, your pension plans, your IRAs, and your 401(k)s with no unrelated business taxable income, no UBTI. The tax matrix can be examined in detail in Appendix D.

The conversation about REITs could be a full book to itself, but we couldn't end this discussion without covering at least the basics. The bottom line: by providing a reliable income vehicle with growth and inflation protection, REITs have become a solution for millions of Americans, providing desirable portfolio diversification in a hard asset that tends to increase over time. That is why REITs should be included in a well-balanced investment portfolio.

Chapter Sixteen
DST-to-UPREIT
Transactions

Essentials

Section 721 is an ordinary provision of the Tax Code dealing with property contributed to a partnership. How does it work? When you contribute property to a partnership in return for interests in the partnership, there is no tax to the contributor or the partnership. Real simple. This becomes interesting when real estate is contributed to the operating partnership (OP) of a REIT, referred to as an umbrella partnership real estate investment trust (UPREIT), as we will discuss. Section 721 operates in a manner similar to Section 1031; Section 721 is another method of deferring gain from investment real estate.

In an UPREIT transaction, the owner contributes their real estate to the operating partnership of a REIT. The contributor then becomes a partner in the REIT's operating partnership. That is a typical UPREIT. There is no gain to the contributor under Section 721. Famous real estate investor, Sam Zell, is best known for the structure after he contributed a large number of properties to his affiliated REIT.

In a DST scenario, DST owners contribute their interests in a DST property to the operating partnership of a REIT in exchange for the REIT's OP units. Again, there is no tax to the contributor under Section 721.

There are numerous benefits to investors in DST-to-UPREIT transactions, including the following:

- No taxable gain, Section 721
- Retention of tax benefits
- An increase in distributions
- A safety net through diversification
- An ability to improve the property to capture future appreciation
- A long-term investment vehicle
- Liquidity options
- Lower fees

Terminology

"721 exchange": A 721 exchange permits real estate owners (including DST owners) to contribute their property to a partnership in exchange for interests in that partnership on a tax-deferred basis.

"Umbrella partnership real estate investment trust" (UPREIT): An UPREIT is a REIT that allows owners of real estate to contribute their property in exchange for operating partnership interests in the REIT.

"Operating partnership" (OP): REITs typically own their real estate in an operating partnership.

"Operating partnership units" (OP units): These units represent ownership of the OP that owns the REIT's real estate. These units, acquired during a 721 exchange, may be converted into REIT shares (typically on a taxable basis).

A new twist on the traditional REIT is gaining popularity, and it's combining some of my favorite wealth-building strategies. DSTs have become a powerful tool for tax-advantaged real estate investing under Section 1031, as you know.

However, there are many structural requirements for a DST to qualify for Section 1031 treatment. For example, DST properties must be sold when their mortgage matures, and it is not permissible to recapitalize or refinance a DST property, even when it would be in the best interest of the owners. This means that DST properties typically must be sold every ten years when their mortgage matures, even if the owners are happy with their property or it's a bad time to sell. Thus, DSTs provide tax deferral, but to maintain that deferral, the DST owners must exchange over and over again.

By contrast, **DST owners who participate in an UPREIT transaction obtain permanent tax deferral and ultimately tax exclusion (tax forgiveness) if they hold the investment until death.** How? By participating in an UPREIT transaction, DST owners obtain permanent tax deferral by exchanging their DST interests for OP units in a REIT. In addition, those DST owners obtain tax exclusion by holding their OP units until death, at which point their heirs obtain the basis step up we discussed in earlier chapters. Let's discuss the details.

These DST structural concerns, and a number of additional REIT benefits, have sparked a new progression: the DST-to-UPREIT transaction. When a DST property matures and is ready for sale, the DST owners may contribute their interests in the DST, which had until this time been a part of a DST's fractional ownership model, to the operating partnership of a REIT. This is referred to as an UPREIT transaction or a Section 721 exchange, referring to the applicable section of the Tax Code. In the simplest of terms, this permits DST owners to transform their fractional ownership of a single property into a larger REIT portfolio comprising the DST property being contributed plus the REIT's larger property portfolio. DST investors transform their investment from a single property to an interest in a larger, more diversified portfolio. At a high level, these are the basics.

In case you're curious, it is not possible to Section 1031 exchange directly into a REIT like Capital Square Housing Trust. DST-to-UPREIT transactions must be done in two steps. First, an investor would Section 1031 exchange into a qualifying replacement property. **DSTs, as you know, qualify as like-kind replacement property under a Revenue Ruling. But interests in a partnership are not like kind to real estate.** Congress amended Section 1031 back in 1984 to eliminate partnership interests from 1031 exchange treatment.

So, we do the two steps: first 1031 exchange into a DST, and later, typically after two years, the DST owners contribute interests in the DST to the operating partnership in exchange for the REIT's operating partnership interests, so-called "OP units." This is done under Section 721, and there is no tax to the contributor.

Let's explore these DST-to-UPREIT transactions. Like many other forms of real estate investment, education is the key to unlocking transformational wealth potential.

I've seen it happen repeatedly, and it never loses the excitement. For example, we had a DST property in Virginia Beach, Virginia that was approaching maturity; the property was ready to be sold at a large profit. Capital Square Housing Trust, our REIT, offered to buy the property from the DST owners at 100% of appraised value for cash or OP units, at the owner's election. This Class A, 229-unit multifamily community stood less than one mile from the Virginia Beach boardwalk. It's a gated community, featuring a resident clubhouse, controlled-access buildings, a resort-style swimming pool, twenty-four-hour fitness center, dog park, covered parking, and garages–all this across twenty-four acres in an irreplaceable location with very strong economics.

To retain the property long term, Capital Square Housing Trust sought to acquire it, either by contribution from the DST owners or purchase. The property was appraised, and the DST owners were given the benefit of 161% appreciation in value, either in OP units or cash, at each owner's election. Capital Square's award-winning investor relations team encouraged DST investors to work with their financial advisors to select the course that was best for them.

The vast majority elected to participate in a DST-to-UPREIT transaction. A small number elected to swap till they dropped, Section 1031 exchanging their DST investment mostly for another DST selected from Capital Square's portfolio of available replacement properties. A very small number elected to cash out. Typically, this would be taxable, but during the holding period, several investors had died, leaving their heirs with stepped-up basis and the ability to sell without taxation; so, they sold.

We educated our investors. We walked them through the possibilities. Each DST owner was given freedom to choose the path that was best for them. In this case, 85% of DST investors elected to move their investment over to the REIT. By combining favorable tax treatment with increased cash flow, greater diversification, and many REIT benefits, the UPREIT transaction was an overwhelming success in spite of the challenges in the economy in 2023.

Note: REITs typically hold their real estate in an operating partnership (OP) that owns many properties. This is done in large part to give the contributors the benefit of favorable partnership tax treatment along with property diversification. Instead of owning a single property (or a single DST), the contributor becomes a partner in a multi-asset partnership that is operated by the REIT, creating greater property diversification and numerous other REIT benefits.

Taking this back one step further, REITs use the OP structure to obtain favorable partnership tax treatment for contributors. This means that contributors are still owners of real estate and still obtain the many tax benefits, including tax deductions for depreciation and operating expenses, that help shelter their distributions from taxation.

Here's how it works: an UPREIT transaction permits real estate owners to contribute their property to the REIT's

operating partnership in exchange for interests in that partnership on a tax-deferred basis. Under Section 721, there is no gain to the contributor (the property owner) or the recipient (the operating partnership). An UPREIT transaction allows a property owner to exchange one property for ownership in a larger, more diversified portfolio that is professionally managed by the REIT. In the DST scenario, an UPREIT transaction allows a DST owner to exchange their interests in a DST for ownership in the REIT's larger, more diversified, professionally managed portfolio. Simple. The operating partnership may assume the contributor's debt or repay it at closing, but there is no rule similar to the Section 1031 debt replacement requirement, which is nice.

Some DST sponsors have mandatory UPREITs, and others are voluntary, like at Capital Square. In a mandatory UPREIT, the sponsor's affiliated REIT has the option to call the DST interests on pre-established terms–typically two years after closing. Upon calling the DST interest, the investor is required to complete an UPREIT transaction for operating partnership (OP) units. The UPREIT is mandatory.

In a voluntary UPREIT, which is how Capital Square works through the process, the DST owner is given the choice of investing the current fair market value of his or her DST interests in the operating partnership. Alternatively, the DST owner could use the proceeds to do another Section 1031 exchange or cash out on a taxable basis. Personally, I believe voluntary UPREITs should be encouraged to give investors the maximum flexibility when it comes to their reinvestment options. Mandatory UPREITs seem wrong to me. How is an investor to make an informed investment decision today when the UPREIT transaction will not occur for two years in the future? And in this case, the investor would be unable to say, "no," even if the REIT is no longer a desirable investment.

Of course, I also believe there's potential for tremendous value when investors elect to participate in DST-to-UPREIT transactions. Considering the 85% of DST investors in the Virginia Beach multifamily property I mentioned, as a result of the $72 million UPREIT transaction, these DST investors realized an approximately 161% total return. Then, their tax-advantaged real estate investment continued to do its work with greater diversification, tax sheltered cash flow, and permanent tax deferral.

This leads us to the tax ramifications. Section 721 is a very common provision dealing with entities taxed as partnerships. It provides that when the owner contributes property to a partnership in return for interests in the partnership, there is no taxable gain to the contributor or the partnership. Again, very simple.

Section 721 deals with partnership contributions, and Section 1031 governs tax-deferred real estate exchanges. They could not be more different in their purpose, but they operate in a very similar manner.

How so?

Both involve tax deferral and carry over basis. There is no immediate taxation on partnership contributions under 721, just like there is no immediate taxation with a 1031 exchange. In both cases, the tax basis carries over, and the tax is deferred until the partnership interest is sold in a taxable transaction. The same is true with Section 1031 exchanges, where the exchanger's tax basis carries over to their replacement property. The tax is deferred until the replacement property is sold in a taxable transaction. The contribution of DST replacement property to an UPREIT is not a taxable sale; it is a tax-free contribution under Section 721, with the tax deferred. The former DST owner has the ability to obtain permanent tax deferral and ultimately tax forgiveness by holding their interests until death without the need for future exchanges. Mission accomplished for perpetual tax deferral.

Regarding timing, Section 1031 has a number of timelines: forty-five days to identify, 180 days to close. Section 721 does not have any statutory timelines. There is no qualified intermediary or Exchange Agreement, and there is no debt replacement requirement. Section 721 operates simply and easily.

But examples help, so let me share another.

As a result of a $26.9 million UPREIT transaction of one of Capital Square's other multifamily communities–this one in Athens, Georgia–the DST owners who participated realized a 226% total return (distributions plus profits) and an equity multiple of over 1.85% (profit without distributions). And again, their investment in real estate continued after this favorable transaction, providing tax-sheltered cash flow.

The UPREIT structure is also beneficial for estate planning and gifting because OP units can be divided for distribution to heirs or partners. Then, each individual OP holder can make their own decision whether to hold or sell some of the OP units in the future. For example, if an individual owns OP units and dies, the heirs can divide the OP units as a part of settling the estate. If the OP units are owned by a partnership, the OP units can be divided among the partners, and the partnership oftentimes can be liquidated.

There are many potential benefits to DST owners who participate in a DST-to-UPREIT transaction, including:

- **No taxable gain:** Under Section 721, DST owners will not recognize any taxable gain. Most DST owners acquired their DST interests in a tax-deferred exchange under Section 1031. At every property sale, each DST owner must structure another exchange to continue their tax deferral. However, by participating in an UPREIT transaction, DST owners will have the ability to make this tax deferral permanent by holding their OP units until death.

- **Retention of tax benefits:** Owners will continue to receive the tax benefits of real estate ownership, including deductions for depreciation and operating expenses, that will shelter OP distributions from taxation.

- **Increase in distributions:** Distributions from the OP increase and will continue to be paid monthly via direct deposit.

- **A safety net through diversification:** Participating DST owners will have the safety net of a more diversified investment because the OP owns a larger portfolio of multifamily properties. The OP structure provides safety through increased property diversification, reducing the risk of loss.

- **Ability to improve the property to capture future appreciation:** Many DST properties will benefit from additional capital improvements to further increase value beyond the funds in the DST's reserves. The DST tax structure does not permit refinancing or recapitalizing to upgrade a property, even if this would add value and benefit the DST owners. REITs typically have capital to upgrade properties, adding value and increasing cash flow.

- **Long-term hold:** The DST properties being considered for the REIT are quality assets that should be held long term for increased cash flow and appreciation. However, the DST tax structure does not permit a longer-term hold; the tax rules require a sale when the current loan matures. The OP structure does not have this requirement, which means that participating DST owners will enjoy the economic benefits of the property and the OP's other properties on a long-term basis.

- **Liquidity option:** The OP is intended to provide a liquidity option that is not possible under the DST structure.

- **Transparency:** The REIT also provides a high degree of transparency with a majority of independent board members and financial statements audited by a national accounting firm, plus greater access to capital markets and funding options.

- **Low fees:** Capital Square's REIT, Capital Square Housing Trust, has very low fees to maximize cash flow to participating DST owners.

In conclusion, real estate investment structures evolve over time. From a rental house to a TIC, a TIC to a DST, and now DST-to-UPREIT transactions, real estate investments trend toward higher quality, investment-grade properties. DST-to-UPREIT transactions are the latest structure that provides positive tax and financial benefits for real estate owners. My favorite wealth-building strategies just keep getting better and better.

Chapter Seventeen
Reflections on Building Family Wealth while Minimizing Taxes

As you've read this book, I hope you have learned how to build family wealth while minimizing taxes and maximizing returns through real estate investments. I hope you have had fun with 1031 and learned more about how you can "swap till ya' drop." You've also learned how we are an investor-centric company at Capital Square. Everything we do is with investors in mind.

We've been winning all kinds of awards lately. It's wild. Capital Square has been recognized by Inc. 5000 as one of the fastest-growing companies in the nation for eight consecutive years now and among the top 100 "Inspiring Global Workplaces." The most unexpected award was being named among GlobeSt. Real Estate Forum's "Best Bosses" in 2020. I am the best boss. I mean, none of you reading this work for me, so who's to say? But I like that one.

I was born in a small town. Think of the John Cougar song, "Small Town," but my small town was Smithfield, Virginia, home of the world-famous Smithfield hams. My family was very active in local theatre. You could say that we were the original Smithfield hams. But I should start further back than this.

After immigrating through Ellis Island, my great-grandparents had a tiny store in Brooklyn, the kind that sold bread and milk to the neighbors for two cents each. My family lived above the store in very simple accommodations–no hot water, four to a room. As I talk about Capital Square's acquisition of nearly $8 billion of real estate and write these words from a beautiful farm in Hanover County, Virginia, it's hard to imagine my family's humble roots.

As a result of being crammed into that tiny Brooklyn apartment, several members of the younger generation developed a love of wide-open spaces, the country, and the animals you could have there. A number of veterinarians followed down the line, including my own father. As a large animal vet, my dad cared for thousands of large and small animals, including many hogs that became Smithfield hams.

My brother followed the same path, but I didn't. I was antsy to get out of Smithfield and out of that small world. I went to college at Northeastern University in Boston, hunkering down and graduating as president of the student government, just one mark short of a perfect 4.0 record. It's funny; in my day, Northeastern had open admissions, so virtually anyone could attend. But the dean told us at the first convocation, "Look to your right and look to your left. One of you won't be here after Christmas."

Today, Northeastern is an excellent school; I got an upgrade.

Heading into senior year, I asked the constitutional law professor, "What is the greatest law school in the world?"

"Oxford, of course," he replied.

"But I don't want to go to Mississippi."

He laughed before clarifying, "Oxford University in England."

I nodded. That made sense. Fast forward a half year or so. In 1979, I landed at Wadham College, Oxford University, in England, an aspiring scholar on a cheap flight from Boston. The day was cold, and the newspaper headlines read, "Prime Minister Thatcher doubles tuition on foreign students." A bad recession dragged on in England, which didn't make a great start for an American student in Oxford, but I knew the value of education.

I was starting to learn how the right strategies combined with hard work and a little luck make all the difference.

Oxford is composed of over thirty independent colleges. You live, study, and play in your college and only come together for final exams at the end. My college, Wadham, was formed back in 1610 and had an excellent law faculty. Wadham uses the tutorial method, where two students meet weekly with the don (professor) to review the course materials, ending each session by reading a paper you have written on a topic of interest. This was somewhat intimidating for a kid from Smithfield and even worse when Professor Hackney referred to me pejoratively as a "North American" or ridiculed my friend, Jon, for his "Welsh homespun jurisprudence," which was code for not being prepared and making things up on the fly.

Because I had my undergraduate degree from Northeastern, I was able to complete the Oxford law degree in only two years, skipping the first year entirely and jumping into the deep end of the Oxford law curriculum. My B.A. Jurisprudence with Honors was later upgraded to an M.A. Jurisprudence after attending a sort of dinner party in the college called a "gaudie." So, great. I had two degrees from Oxford. Then, after returning Stateside, my next goal was University of Virginia Law School. Again, because I had an Oxford law degree, I completed law school in only two years at UVA. This was on a Friday in the spring of 1984. My exams ended, and I headed to work in Richmond, Virginia the next Monday, and you've heard the rest of this story.

By the early 1990s, I was giving a lot of talks on Section 1031 exchanges and related topics. I would talk to anyone who would hear me: lawyers, accountants, broker-dealers, and regular folks. At the same time, I was writing articles on tax topics for publication in any magazine, journal, periodical, or paper that would have me. During this time, a distant family relation on my mom's side through marriage, named Steven, was a securities broker-dealer with H. Beck/Capital Financial Group in Bethesda, Maryland. Steven was very interested in what we were doing with 1031 and

TICs. But this was very, very early on, around 1991 or 1992. TICs were not yet an industry.

Steven was focused on helping his representatives solve tax issues for investors who owned appreciated real estate and would have a large tax to pay upon sale. He supported educating his representatives on Section 1031 and TICs as a way to defer the taxes by acquiring quality replacement property. TICs were a solution for the firm's investors who had tax issues and wanted a turn-key solution.

I spoke to the firm's representatives regularly, as often as they would let me. I also sent them articles I was writing on various tax topics. Over time, Steven saw that we were gaining momentum with his representatives and realized I was an authority in this emerging space. Through various relationships, Steven recommended me to the man who would be the future founder of Triple Net Properties in Orange County, California. That was very fortunate and, as you will learn, changed the trajectory of my career and life. This was a very lucky turn of events, but perhaps it was not pure luck. What did the winningest UCLA basketball coach, John Wooden, say about luck? To paraphrase Wooden, the harder you work, the more luck you will have; and luck is the result of preparation meeting opportunity.

Triple Net ultimately hired me as outside legal counsel to create the first TIC programs, REITs, and real estate funds, and ultimately, I became their president many years later, living in "So Cal" when Triple Net was the most prolific TIC syndicator in the nation. Goodbye, buttoned-down lawyer life in Richmond, Virginia. Hello, California dreaming and a Mercedes AMG sports car with a V-12 engine. But if Steven had not mentioned my work to that syndicator in California, it might not have happened. I could be a retired lawyer now but for that introduction back in the dark days of the 1990s as a result of giving seminars and writing articles on tax topics. Perhaps John Wooden would say this was preparation meeting opportunity.

When Triple Net Properties was founded, I formed it as a Virginia Limited Liability Company–yes, a California company was formed as a Virginia LLC for the many benefits of the Virginia LLC statute and Virginia law. And we formed hundreds of Virginia LLCs as the entity of choice for real estate ownership.

During my first day on the job in California, Sylvia, the unflappable receptionist said, "The sheriff is here for you."

"The sheriff?" I didn't know what the heck was going on. Did I do something wrong? Was this some crazy California thing? It turned out the sheriff was there to take my fingerprints, a customary part of my FINRA application to be licensed as a securities broker-dealer, and ultimately president of the firm's broker-dealer.

Not long after, I received a package in the mail that sounded like a ticking bomb. Tick tick tick. Triple Net had thousands of investors. Was one of them unhinged for some reason? The bomb squad was called. They opened the box. And inside was a chattering teeth wind-up toy sent to me from a competitor. Only in California.

California is known for many things, some good and some not so good. California is definitely known for real estate. Californians love their real estate. Through the generations, California real estate has proven to be the source of great wealth, the bedrock for many residents' net worth.

Real estate appreciates most rapidly on the nation's coasts, and California real estate seems to appreciate like a rocket ship with nearly unlimited potential. This rapid appreciation in value plus the punitive tax rates in California have made Section 1031 common knowledge and a common practice for even regular folks in the Golden State.

While the TIC program was created in large part in Richmond, Virginia at Hirschler Fleischer, my old law firm, the East Coast did not take much notice. Even Section 1031 that had been in the Tax Code since 1921 was hardly known, especially in my home state of Virginia, where the old guard often had the mentality that "if

my granddaddy didn't know about exchanging, it wasn't for me."
But in the West–California especially–exchanges and TICs
became commonplace.

When I lived there, leading the nation's largest sponsor of
alternative real estate investments, I once was in line at Gelson's,
a fancy grocery store off the coastal highway in Laguna Beach,
back around 2008 or 2009. Right next to me, one soccer mom
waiting for her take-out order said to another soccer mom,
"My TIC is going full cycle this month," and the other answered,
"My TIC is not going full cycle until next year." At the time, TICs
were still largely unknown in the East.

It was a whole new world in California, and I loved it–though
in time, Virginia and its rural spaces called me home.

As a sponsor at Capital Square these days, I talk to a lot of
Section 1031 exchange investors, including many from California.
The conversation is typically about the DST program and how
it works, along with the opportunity to invest in the vibrant
Southeastern real estate market. There are so many advantages
in the Southeast. I should know, having lived here most of my
life, witnessing the evolution of cities and towns into new twen-
ty-first-century versions of themselves. There has truly been a
migration from the gateway cities to the suburban markets in the
Southeast. Why? Because the Southeast is blessed with a combination of excellent paying jobs, lower cost of living, higher quality of
life, mild weather, and lower rates of crime in a less dense, suburban
environment that proved to be desirable during the pandemic and
still is highly desirable today to millions of residents moving into
the region. Just track U-Hauls; they go one way from the gateway
cities to the Southeast and not the other way.[xviii] To quote Charlie
Daniels in his rebellious song, "The South is going to do it again."
The Southeast has done it again and again as a prime market for
real estate investments.

My work and my life have always kept me on my toes, but
they have also allowed me to play a role in the empowerment of
countless people's lives. I tell you all this because opportunities

abound for each of us. As the great-grandson of dirt-poor immigrants and a family line that has faced adversity as far back as I know, I stand today as the result of generations of hard work, discipline, and pursuit of a better life. Fingerprints happen. Chattering teeth happen. But so does transformation.

In 2012, I cashed out of my lawyer retirement account to form Capital Square. The past thirteen years have been a phenomenal run, from a small group that had worked together previously at other sponsor firms to the over 350 employees we have today. The growth has been exceptional. We work hard, live modestly, and have reinvested the firm's profits every year to grow.

It's a familiar refrain that we want the next generation to be better off than our own, and I am honored to help investors with this every single day. And I am honored to work with trusted family members, a son-in-law as co-CEO, a daughter as COO, and a second daughter who oversees debt as a managing director at one of the nation's leading real estate loan originators. It is the highlight of my life to work with trusted loved ones on our most important mission.

As for myself, someday I will be done swapping and will be the one dropping. Think of the 1970 Billboard hit song, "Spirit in the Sky." Then, my kids are going to get the step up in basis on my real estate. Maybe my daughters will buy a Lamborghini or something frivolous. No, I'm kidding. They won't. They get it. They understand the value of building family wealth over time. They have their own families now.

To sum up, when you need tax-advantaged wealth strategies, real estate can galvanize everything you've worked for, emboldening your family's future wealth by minimizing taxes and, at the same time, maximizing returns. This could be a Section 1031 tax-deferred exchange, such as a Delaware statutory trust (DST), or a qualified opportunity zone (QOZ) fund for tax deferral and exclusion of capital gains from the sale of any asset. It could be a development fund for higher returns in a shorter holding period or a real estate investment trust (REIT), such as Capital Square Housing Trust, for stable income, growth, and inflation protection.

As one of the nation's leading sponsors of tax-advantaged real estate investments, Capital Square builds legacies for investors, team members, and communities–enabling the discovery and implementation of tax-advantaged real estate investments with unwavering integrity, developing best-in-class multifamily communities synonymous with value, and managing multifamily properties with a drive for excellence.

In short, "Invest, Build, Manage" results in "Income, Growth, and Tax-efficiency." Thinking about your past, your present, and your possibilities for the future is easier when you can position the scaffolding that maintains the whole.

"Swap till ya' drop" is both a transformative financial strategy and an existential reality check. I wish you all the best wherever the journey takes you.

Acronym Guide

BFR: Build for rent
DD: Due diligence
DDO: Due diligence officer
DDQ: Due diligence questionnaire
DST: Delaware statutory trust
FINRA: The Financial Industry Regulatory Authority
LTV: Loan-to-value
MF: Multifamily
MHC: Manufactured housing community
MOB: Medical office building
OP: Operating partnership
OZ: Opportunity zone
PA: Purchase Agreement
PLR: Private Letter Ruling
PPM: Private placement memorandum
PQ: Purchaser questionnaire
QI: Qualified intermediary
QOZ: Qualified opportunity zone
REIT: Real estate investment trust
RIA: Registered investment advisor
SEC: The U.S. Securities and Exchange Commission
SFR: Single-family rental
TIC: Tenants in common
UBTI: Unrelated business taxable income
UPREIT: Umbrella partnership real estate investment trust

Glossary of Terms

"Accredited investor" – An investor that is deemed financially sophisticated and qualified to invest in private (unregistered) securities by satisfying income or net-worth standards established by the SEC

"Actual receipt" – Taking possession of the funds received from a sale (see related: "constructive receipt")

"Appreciation" – The increase in an asset's value

"Basis" – The metric used to compute depreciation deductions and taxable gain on sale

"Beneficial interests" – The interests the investors own in a DST

"Boot" – Items that do not qualify for Section 1031 tax deferral, including cash received, debt reduction, and other non-like-kind property received in an exchange

"Constructive receipt" – Funds received by a taxpayer via a third-party agent (see related: "actual receipt")

"Current return" – The cash flow from an investment (compare to: "appreciation" and "profit")

"Deferred exchange" – An exchange in which the replacement property is acquired after the taxpayer transfers the relinquished property

"Delaware statutory trust" (DST) – A legal entity allowing investors to acquire fractional ownership of real estate, without being responsible for management, in a structure that qualifies for Section 1031 exchange treatment

"Delayed exchange" (see: "deferred exchange")

"De-leverage" – To reduce debt

"DST" (see: "Delaware statutory trust)

"Equity multiple" – The ratio of profit to the original equity invested, typically stated as a percentage, for example, 2x Equity Multiple, which means that the profit on sale equates to two times the equity invested

"Exchange accommodator" (see: "Qualified intermediary")

"Exchange Agreement" – A written contract defining the terms of an exchange

"Exit LTV" – The loan-to-value (LTV) ratio at the time of a relinquished property's closing, which is the amount of debt required on the replacement property to fully qualify for exchange treatment (see related: "Loan-to-Value (LTV) Ratio")

"Gross lease" – An ownership structure where the owner/landlord is responsible for expenses (see related: "net lease")

"High-leverage DST" – A Delaware statutory trust with a higher-than-normal amount of debt in place (see related: "low-leverage DST")

"Holding period" – The time during which an investment is held

"Improved real estate" – A parcel of land on which improvements have been constructed (see related: "unimproved real estate")

"Investment-grade real estate"– The highest quality real estate, typically too large and too expensive for individual investors to acquire on their own

"Leverage" – The placing of debt on a property; borrowing to pay for a portion of the purchase price

"Loan-to-value (LTV) ratio" – The relationship between money borrowed (debt) and the value of the asset

"Low-leverage DST" – A Delaware statutory trust with a lower-than-normal amount of debt in place (see related: "high-leverage DST")

"LTV" (see: "Loan-to-Value ratio" and "Exit LTV")

"Net lease" – A passive ownership structure frequently used for investment real estate, where the tenant bears most property expenses, as opposed to the owner/landlord (see related: "gross lease")

"Operating partnership" (OP) – The operating structure of a real estate investment trust in which the real estate is held

"Operating partnership units" (OP units) – Fractional ownership of the operating partnership that owns the real estate investment trust's real estate

"Opportunity zone" (see: "qualified opportunity zone")

"Private Letter Ruling" (PLR) – A private ruling issued by the IRS/Treasury at the request of a specific taxpayer on a matter of tax law; represents authority binding on that taxpayer alone and is not intended to constitute a matter of substantive law

"Profit" – The appreciation or profit on sale of an investment

"OZ" (see: "qualified opportunity zone")

"Qualified intermediary" (QI) – An entity or individual who facilitates Section 1031 exchanges, helping the exchanger qualify for a safe harbor, supporting a taxpayer's intent to carry out a Section 1031 exchange

"Qualified opportunity zone" (QOZ) – Designated census tracts created as a part of the Tax Cuts and Jobs Act of 2017 to stimulate long-term private investments in low-income urban and rural communities across the United States and five U.S. territories

"Real estate investment trust" (REIT) – A company that invests in or finances income-producing real estate

"Relinquished property" – A taxpayer's existing property that is being disposed of in a Section 1031 exchange (see related: "replacement property")

"Replacement property" – A taxpayer's new property to be acquired in a Section 1031 exchange (see related: "relinquished property")

"Revenue Procedure" (Rev. Proc.) – An IRS/Treasury statement of the requirements necessary to apply for a ruling; not a statement of substantive law

"Revenue Ruling" (Rev. Rul.) – A published ruling from the IRS/Treasury on a matter of tax law; represents authority binding on all taxpayers and is a statement of substantive law

"Safe harbor" – A provision that avoids or eliminates legal or regulatory uncertainty

"Section 721 exchange" – A tax-advantaged transaction following a provision in the Tax Code that permits real estate owners (including DST owners) to contribute their property to the operating partnership of a real estate investment trust (REIT) in exchange for interests in that partnership on a tax-deferred basis

"Section 1031 exchange" – A tax-advantaged transaction following a provision in the Tax Code that permits real estate investors to defer capital gains taxes on the sale of real property by reinvesting the proceeds in like-kind real estate

"Simultaneous exchange" – An exchange in which the relinquished and replacement properties close simultaneously (compare to: "delayed exchange")

"Tax deferral" – Delaying the required payment of taxes

"Tax exclusion" – Eliminating the required payment of taxes

"Tenants in Common" (TIC) – A fractional ownership structure, utilizing Section 1031 of the Tax Code to permit fractional ownership of real estate (compare to: "Delaware statutory trust")

"Total return" – The metric used to assess the success of a given real estate investment, computed at the end of the holding period when the property is sold, based on (1) total distributions (cash flow) plus (2) profit (appreciation) on sale (compare to: "current return" and "profit")

"Umbrella partnership real estate investment trust" (UPREIT) – A REIT structure that allows owners of real estate to exchange their property for operating partnership units in the REIT

"Unimproved real estate" – Real estate on which no structures have been built, commonly referred to as land (see related: "improved real estate")

"Vesting" – The moment in time when legal ownership of a property is officially transferred from seller to buyer

Appendix A:
Internal Revenue Code Section 1031

"No gain or loss shall be recognized on the exchange of real property held for productive use in a trade or business or for investment if such real property is exchanged solely for real property of like kind which is to be held either for productive use in a trade or business or for investment."

Appendix B: Section 1031 Regulations

The following text is excerpted from the Treasury Regulations on Section 1031:

§ 1.1031(a)—1 Property held for productive use in trade or business or for investment.

(a) In general—(1) *Exchanges of property solely for property of a like kind.* Section 1031(a)(1) provides an exception from the general rule requiring the recognition of gain or loss upon the sale or exchange of property. Under Section 1031(a)(1), no gain or loss is recognized if property held for productive use in a trade or business or for investment is exchanged solely for property of a like kind to be held either for productive use in a trade or business or for investment. Under Section 1031(a)(1), property held for productive use in a trade or business may be exchanged for property held for investment. Similarly, under Section 1031(a)(1), property held for investment may be exchanged for property held for productive use in a trade or business. However, Section 1031(a)(2) provides that Section 1031(a)(1) does not apply to any exchange of—

(i) Stock in trade or other property held primarily for sale;

(ii) Stocks, bonds, or notes;

(iii) Other securities or evidences of indebtedness or interest;

(iv) Interests in a partnership;

(v) Certificates of trust or beneficial interests; or

(vi) Choses in action.

Section 1031(a)(1) does not apply to any exchange of interests in a partnership regardless of whether the interests exchanged are general or limited partnership interests or are interests in the same partnership or in different partnerships. An interest in a partnership that has in effect a valid election under Section 761(a) to be excluded from the application of all of subchapter K is treated as an interest in each of the assets of the partnership and not as an interest in a partnership for purposes of Section 1031(a)(2)(D) and paragraph (a)(1)(iv) of this Section. An exchange of an interest in such a partnership does not qualify for nonrecognition of gain or loss under Section 1031 with respect to any asset of the partnership that is described in Section 1031(a)(2) or to the extent the exchange of assets of the partnership does not otherwise satisfy the requirements of Section 1031(a).

(2) *Exchanges of property not solely for property of a like kind.* A transfer is not within the provisions of Section 1031(a) if, as part of the consideration, the taxpayer receives money or property which does not meet the requirements of Section 1031(a), but the transfer, if otherwise qualified, will be within the provisions of either Section 1031 (b) or (c). Similarly, a transfer is not within the provisions of Section 1031(a) if, as part of the consideration, the other party to the exchange assumes a liability of the taxpayer (or acquires property from the taxpayer that is subject to a liability), but the transfer, if otherwise qualified, will be within the provisions of either Section 1031 (b) or (c). A transfer of property meeting the requirements of Section 1031(a) may be within the provisions of Section 1031(a) even though the taxpayer transfers in addition property not meeting the requirements of Section 1031(a) or money. However, the nonrecognition treatment provided by Section 1031(a) does not apply to the property transferred which does not meet the requirements of Section 1031(a).

(3) *Exchanges after 2017.* Pursuant to Section 13303 of Public Law 115-97 (131 Stat. 2054), for exchanges beginning after December 31, 2017, Section 1031 and §§ 1.1031(a)-1, 1.1031(b)-2, 1.1031(d)-1T, 1.1031(d)-2, 1.1031(j)-1, 1.1031(k)-1, and references to Section 1031 in §§ 1.1031(b)-1, 1.1031(c)-1, and 1.1031(d)-1, apply only to qualifying exchanges of real property (within the meaning of § 1.1031(a)-3) that is held for productive use in a trade or business, or for investment, and that is not held primarily for sale.

(b) *Definition of "like kind."* As used in Section 1031(a), the words like kind have reference to the nature or character of the property and not to its grade or quality. One kind or class of property may not, under that Section, be exchanged for property of a different kind or class. The fact that any real estate involved is improved or unimproved is not material, for that fact relates only to the grade or quality of the property and not to its kind or class. Unproductive real estate held by one other than a dealer for future use or future realization of the increment in value is held for investment and not primarily for sale. For additional rules for exchanges of personal property, see § 1.1031 (a)-2.

(c) *Examples of exchanges of property of a "like kind."* No gain or loss is recognized if (1) a taxpayer exchanges property held for productive use in his trade or business, together with cash, for other property of like kind for the same use, such as a truck for a new truck or a passenger automobile for a new passenger automobile to be used for a like purpose; or (2) a taxpayer who is not a dealer in real estate exchanges city real estate for a ranch or farm, or exchanges a leasehold of a fee with 30 years or more to run for real estate, or exchanges improved real estate for unimproved real estate; or (3) a taxpayer exchanges investment property and cash for investment property of a like kind.

(2) *Exchanges after 2017.* The provisions of paragraph (a)(3) of this Section apply to exchanges beginning after December 2, 2020

Appendix C: IRS Form 8824
(to report a 1031 exchange)

Form **8824**	**Like-Kind Exchanges**	OMB No. 1545-1190
Department of the Treasury Internal Revenue Service	**(and section 1043 conflict-of-interest sales)** Attach to your tax return. Go to *www.irs.gov/Form8824* for instructions and the latest information.	**2024** Attachment Sequence No. **109**

Name(s) shown on tax return	Identifying number

Part I Information on the Like-Kind Exchange

Note: Only real property should be described on lines 1 and 2. If the property described on line 1 or line 2 is real property located outside the United States, indicate the country.

1 Description of like-kind property given up:

2 Description of like-kind property received:

3 Date like-kind property given up was originally acquired (month, day, year) . . . . | **3** | MM/DD/YYYY

4 Date you actually transferred your property to the other party (month, day, year) . . . . . . | **4** | MM/DD/YYYY

5 Date like-kind property you received was identified by written notice to another party (month, day, year). See instructions for 45-day written identification requirement . . . . | **5** | MM/DD/YYYY

6 Date you actually received the like-kind property from other party (month, day, year). See instructions . . . . | **6** | MM/DD/YYYY

7 Was the exchange of the property given up or received made with a related party, either directly or indirectly (such as through an intermediary)? See instructions. If "Yes," complete Part II. If "No," go to Part III . . . . ☐ Yes ☐ No

Note: Do not file this form if a related party sold property into the exchange, directly or indirectly (such as through an intermediary); that property became your replacement property, and none of the exceptions on line 11 applies to the exchange. Instead, report the disposition of the property as if the exchange had been a sale. If one of the exceptions on line 11 applies to the exchange, complete Part II.

Part II Related Party Exchange Information

8	Name of related party	Relationship to you	Related party's identifying number
	Address (no., street, and apt., room, or suite no.; city or town; state; and ZIP code)		

9 During this tax year (and before the date that is 2 years after the last transfer of property that was part of the exchange), did the related party sell or dispose of any part of the like-kind property received from you (or an intermediary) in the exchange? . . . . ☐ Yes ☐ No

10 During this tax year (and before the date that is 2 years after the last transfer of property that was part of the exchange), did you sell or dispose of any part of the like-kind property you received? . . . . . . ☐ Yes ☐ No

*If both lines 9 and 10 are "No" and this is the year of the exchange, go to Part III. If both lines 9 and 10 are "No" and this is **not** the year of the exchange, stop here. If either line 9 or line 10 is "Yes," complete Part III and report on this year's tax return the deferred gain or (loss) from line 24 **unless** one of the exceptions on line 11 applies.*

11 If one of the exceptions below applies to the disposition, check the applicable box.

a ☐ The disposition was after the death of either of the related parties.

b ☐ The disposition was an involuntary conversion, and the threat of conversion occurred after the exchange.

c ☐ You can establish to the satisfaction of the IRS that neither the exchange nor the disposition had tax avoidance as one of its principal purposes. If this box is checked, attach an explanation. See instructions.

For Paperwork Reduction Act Notice, see the instructions.	Cat. No. 12311A	Form **8824** (2024)

Appendix D: Tax Matrix

Sale of Real Estate (not principal residence)	Any Capital Gains (including real estate)	Discretionary Cash ($) to Invest		Qualified Funds (tax-exempt pension plans, IRAs, 401(k)s)
Section 1031 Exchange for tax deferral	Opportunity Zone Fund for tax deferral and exclusion | special distribution to pay taxes	REIT | diversified real estate portfolio	Development LLCs | develop new apartment communities	REIT | tax exempt, no tax (no UBTI)
Stable income	Stable income	Stable income	High returns from development	Stable income
Growth	Growth	Growth	Maximum return	Growth
Tax benefits	Tax benefits	Tax benefits	Maximum return	Tax benefits

Appendix E: Estimate the Tax Consequences

Investors have a choice at the end of each DST's lifecycle: cashing out or continuing the investment with another Section 1031 exchange or UPREIT transaction (when applicable).

Cashing Out versus Continuity of Investment

	Cash-Out	Continuity via another Section 1031 exchange or UPREIT
Sale price (no debt)	$1,000,000	$1,000,000
Capital gains taxes due upon sale[1]	$370,000	$0
Proceeds available for future investment[2]	$630,000	$1,000,000

[1]These figures assume a 37% total tax rate from federal and state taxes due on the sale. The tax rate will vary from state to state.
[2]For illustrative purposes only, the cash out proceeds available for investment represents the after-tax cash available for future investment. The proceeds available for investment for the "Section 1031" column represents the amount that would be reinvested in qualifying replacement property in a Section 1031 exchange. Investors who exchange do not receive any cash.

Only one of the above pathways is designed to maximize the growth of wealth.

A Ten-Year Illustration

A taxpayer has already invested available funds in like-kind real estate, such as a DST or an UPREIT transaction: **$1 million**
5% cash flow earned per year: **$50,000**
Over a 10-year holding period, this totals: **$500,000**
Assuming 10% appreciation: **$100,000**
Total Return: $1,600,000

Retained principal, cash flow during the holding period, and realization of the appreciation over time adds up to significant investor gains.

Assume the taxpayer cashed out and chose a different type of investment, beginning with the net after-tax proceeds of $630,000. As you will see, this makes a significant difference:

$630,000 invested in the S&P 500 for 10 years**	$630,000 invested in the Dow Jones Industrial Average for 10 years**
163% growth over a 10-year period (averaging 10.2% annually)[3]	131% growth over a 10-year period (averaging 8.7% annually)[3]
Total Return: $1,026,900	Total Return: $825,300

[3]S&P 500 and Dow Jones Industrial Average growth rate calculated using ten-year data published by Nasdaq.com: Trevor Jennewine, "Here's the Average Stock Market Return Over the Last 10 Years," Nasdaq.com, January 21, 2024.

When comparing ongoing cash flow plus appreciation on deferred taxes through a Section 1031 exchange or UPREIT versus paying capital gains tax, the difference is clear. This is how some of the wealthiest families in the nation grow generational wealth and create legacies.

Appendix F: 1031 Exchanges vs. 1033 Involuntary Conversions

	1031 Exchanges	1033 Involuntary Conversions
Sales Type	Private sale	Involuntary conversions: destruction, theft, government seizure or condemnation, sale under "threat or imminence" of condemnation
Replacement Property Qualifications	"Like-kind" replacement property	"Like-kind" replacement property
Identification Period	45 days	None
Closing Period	Up to 180 days	Up to 3 years after the close of the tax year
Qualified Intermediary	Use a qualified intermediary to obtain the benefit of the safe harbor. Taxpayer MAY NOT receive sale proceeds	No need for a qualified intermediary. Taxpayer MAY receive proceeds, no tracing of funds
Replacement Amount Requirements	Equal or greater value (must reinvest net cash proceeds plus equal or greater debt)	Equal or greater value (may replace equity with debt), no need to escrow or use the actual funds received
Conclusions	Strict Rules: prohibition on receipt of proceeds plus strict identification and replacement period	Liberal Rules: Taxpayer may receive proceeds and reinvest later

Appendix G: DST Tax Opinion Example

The following tax opinion example applies facts to law to reach a "Should Qualify" for 1031 exchange treatment tax opinion.

Note all language within [brackets] is for sample purposes.

Dear [Sponsor]:

[Sponsor Company, LLC] (the "Sponsor"), [High Quality Property, LLC] (the "Signatory Trustee"), and [High Quality Property, DST], a Delaware statutory trust described in Chapter 38 of Title 12 of the Delaware Code (the "Trust"), have retained [Tax Opinion Law Firm, PLC] to address income tax issues in connection with a transaction related to the acquisition of [certain net-leased property] located at [555 High Quality Property Drive].

Specifically, this letter sets forth our opinion as to whether:

- the DST should be treated as an investment trust described in Section 301.7701-4(c) of the Treasury Regulations that is classified as a "trust" under Section 301.7701-4(a) of the Treasury Regulations,

- the owners (the "Beneficial Owners") of beneficial interests in the DST (the "Interests") should be treated as "grantors" of the Trust,

- the Interests should not be treated as a "security" under Section 1031 of the Internal Revenue Code of 1986, as amended (the "Code"), and

- as "grantors," the Beneficial Owners should be treated as acquiring and owning a direct interest in real property for federal income tax purposes. (An Interest must be treated as an interest in real property to qualify as a replacement property under Section 1031.)

Appendix H: TIC vs. DST Structure Comparison

TICs	DSTs	DST Advantages
Only 35 investors	Up to 2,000 investors	**Provides access for more investors**
Higher investment minimums	Lower investment minimums	**Permits smaller investments**
Up to 35 separate real estate closings	Lender only needs to make one loan because the DST owns 100% of the real estate	**Provides simple and more efficient closing investment process (frequently 24-hour turn-around)**
Investors may have some level of personal liability	Loan guarantees apply to sponsors, not investors	**Provides investors protection against personal liability under loans**
All major decisions require unanimous agreement by investors	Sponsor is better equipped to deal with crises than 35 individual TICs	**Empowers the Sponsor to make decisions; Sponsor has the ability to act quickly when issues arise**
Investors can be liable for the actions of their co-investors	Investors cannot cause a default on the loan	**Provides investors greater security against rogue investors**
Each investor must set up an individual LLC	Investors do not need separate LLCs	**Provides a less complex structure for investors**
Lender underwrites each investor	Lender does not underwrite the investors	**Eliminates the need for investors to provide tax returns to lenders**
Only covered by a Revenue Procedure issued by the IRS (Rev. Proc. 2002-22), providing guidance only, not substantive law	Covered by a Revenue Ruling (Rev. Rul. 2004-86), which is a statement of substantive law	**Authorized more formally by the IRS**

Appendix I: Acknowledgment of Beneficial Ownership

Note all language within [brackets] is for sample purposes.

ACKNOWLEDGMENT OF BENEFICIAL OWNERSHIP

[HIGH QUALITY PROPERTY], DST

Escrow No. **[CLOSING FILE NUMBER - HIGH QUALITY PROPERTY]**

[HIGH QUALITY PROPERTY], DST, a Delaware statutory trust, organized under the laws of the State of Delaware (the "Trust"), hereby acknowledges that **[X]** is the owner of a Beneficial Interest equal to **[X]%** of the Beneficial Interests in the Trust, issued pursuant to the Trust Agreement dated as of XX X, 20XX (as may be amended or supplemented from time to time, the "Trust Agreement") by and among [X], LLC, a Delaware limited liability company, as Depositor, [X], LLC, a Delaware limited liability company, as Signatory Trustee, [X], LLC, as Delaware Trustee and [X], as Independent Trustee.

All capitalized terms used in this Acknowledgment and not defined herein shall have the meanings assigned to such terms in the Trust Agreement. Reference is made to the Trust Agreement and any agreements supplemental thereto for a statement of the respective rights and obligations thereunder of the Depositor, the Signatory Trustee, the Delaware Trustee and the Beneficial Owners. This Acknowledgment is subject to all of the terms of the Trust Agreement. Nothing contained in this Acknowledgment shall cause the Beneficial Interest to be deemed a "certificated security" as such term is defined in the Uniform Commercial Code in effect in the jurisdiction in which the Real Estate is located, as amended from time to time.

IN WITNESS WHEREOF, the Trust has caused this Acknowledgment to be signed manually by the Signatory Trustee.

Date: _____

           [HIGH QUALITY PROPERTY], LLC, a Delaware limited liability
           company, not in its individual capacity, but solely as Signatory Trustee
           of the Trust

           By: _____
                    [X], Director

Appendix J: Sample Closing Statement for a DST

Note all language within [brackets] is for sample purposes.

BUYER'S SETTLEMENT STATEMENT

FILE NUMBER:	00XX-PROPERTYX
EST CLOSING DATE:	6/16/2021
SELLER:	[High Quality Property, DST]
BUYER:	X

EQUITY:	$XX,XX...
PROPERTY:	...5 High Qu... ...ge ...tate XXXXX
INTEREST:	0.X...
LTV:	XX.XX%

	CHARGE...	CREDITS
Purchase ...e	X...XX	
Pro-Rata Debt		XXX...X.XX
Funds due from 1031 Excha...		$XX...XX.XX
TOTALS	...XXX.X	$X...XXX.XX

REVIEWED AND APPROVED:

_____   _____
By: Date

_____   _____
By: Date

Appendix K: Photo of ADISA Founders

Left to right: Louis J. Rogers, Tim Snodgrass, Tom Jahncke, Greg Paul, and Bill Winn. Photo Credit: ADISA, 2023.

Acknowledgments

Paula, my trusty wife of over forty years, does all the things on the home front and on Hillbrook Farm, so I can do what I do. We met in 1978 or 1979, when I lived in the Boston apartment where her girlfriend was having a "potty" (Boston-speak for "party"). I said, "hi," and she said, "hi" back. She was cute. There was an immediate attraction, so I invited her to the Bob Dylan concert at the "god'n" (Boston-speak for the "Boston Garden"). She said, "yes." I didn't have tickets, but that was beside the point. Paula has been an active part of my journey from Boston to Oxford to Richmond. Thank you, Paula! None of this would be possible without you.

Special acknowledgements to Jeff Gregor (who said I should write a book a decade ago), Caroline Greber, Shep Haw, and Hunter Lee, valued members of the Capital Square team, who reviewed and commented on the book. I appreciate their thoughts and insights to make the book readable and entertaining. And special thanks to Julia Bard, who was instrumental in the formation of Capital Square and frees me from tedious tasks to have time to write the book and ride horses.

I would like to thank George Howell, Esq. of Hunton & Williams for hiring a boy from Smithfield as a junior tax lawyer, and I would like to acknowledge Dr. Peter Linneman and Willy Walker, leaders in the real estate industry who have inspired me to aim high. I would also like to thank AltsWire (formerly known as The DI Wire) and the publisher, Damon Elder, for their excellent work covering the alternative investment industry, as well as Jill Swartz, partner at Spotlight Marketing Communications. In addition, a big shout out to Mountain Dell Consulting (and their predecessor going back into the TIC era) for reporting on the DST industry statistics. Well done!

Finally, I would like to thank Kris Petroski, Capital Square's VP, Brand Communications, who also served as my book coach and editor. This book would not have happened without her inspiration and perspiration. Thank you, Kris!

About the Author

Louis J. Rogers, the founder and co-chief executive officer of Capital Square and its related entities, began with a vision to build the best real estate investment company possible. He is a nationally recognized authority in structuring securities offerings for real estate investments and serves as a consultant and expert witness on Regulation D private placements, non-traded REITs, Section 1031 exchanges, DST and TIC programs, real estate funds, and issues related to broker-dealers and registered investment advisors. Rogers oversees Capital Square's Delaware statutory trust (DST) programs for investors seeking qualifying replacement property for Section 1031 tax-deferred exchanges. He also provides investment banking services for owners and additionally serves as chairman and chief executive officer of Capital Square Housing Trust, a real estate investment trust (REIT).

From 1987 to 2004, Rogers was a partner with Hirschler Fleischer, a prestigious law firm based in Richmond, Virginia. He founded and led the firm's real estate securities practice group, one of the largest of its kind.

In 1998, Rogers assisted in the formation of Triple Net Properties, LLC as outside legal counsel before being named president and a member of the board in 2004. Under Rogers's leadership, Triple Net became the nation's largest sponsor of securitized Section 1031 exchange programs. While at the firm, he was responsible for the syndication of more than $4 billion of real estate–in excess of 100 offerings, including DSTs, TICs, REITs, and real estate funds that acquired office, government, multifamily, retail, and healthcare properties throughout the United States.

In 2012, Rogers partnered with colleagues he respected from prior firms, seizing their combined expertise across multiple fields to develop a new "investors-first" business model at Capital Square, which is now a vertically aligned real estate company– enabling the discovery and implementation of tax-advantaged real estate investments with unwavering integrity, developing best-in-class multifamily and build-for-rent communities synonymous with value, and managing multifamily properties with a drive for innovation and excellence.

Rogers earned a Bachelor of Science from Northeastern University with highest honors, as well as a Bachelor of Arts with honors and a Master of Arts in jurisprudence from Wadham College, Oxford University. He also earned a juris doctorate from the University of Virginia School of Law. Rogers was a member of the adjunct faculty at the Marshall-Wythe School of Law at the College of William and Mary from 1993 to 1996, and the University of Virginia School of Law from 1995 to 2000, where he taught "Real Estate Transactions and Finance."

Rogers is a founding member of the Tenant in Common Association (TICA)–now known as the Alternative & Direct Investment Securities Association (ADISA)–and served two terms on its board. He also served as chair of the Investment Program Association's Section 1031 Exchange Committee; founding trustee, director, and chair of the Legislative and Regulatory Committee of ADISA; a member of the Board of Governors of the Virginia State Bar, Real Property Section; and a member of the Real Estate Committee of the American Bar Association's Tax Section. Rogers has an AV Peer Review Rating and has been named as one of the top lawyers in Virginia. He has written and lectured widely on real estate, tax, and securities topics and remains active in many bar and real estate security trade groups.

Rogers was a finalist for the 2017 EY Entrepreneur of the Year Mid-Atlantic. In 2020, 2021, 2022, 2023, and 2024, he was listed as one of the most powerful and influential leaders on the Virginia 500 Power List by Virginia Business. He was awarded Real Estate Forum's Best Bosses 2020 by GlobeSt., and in 2022, was not only recognized as an Influencer in Multifamily Real Estate by GlobeSt. Real Estate Forum but was also honored by the National MS Society as the 2022 recipient of the Frank N.

Cowan Silver Hope Award, a recognition of community and humanitarian efforts, given to someone who strives to improve the quality of life today and create a better world tomorrow.

Building legacies for investors, Capital Square team members, and communities continues to drive Louis Rogers's daily work.

Index

[i]David C. Ling and Milena Petrova, "The Tax and Economic Impacts of Section 1031 Like-Kind Exchanges in Real Estate," Real Estate Research Consortium, October 2020.

[ii]ibid.

[iii]"Economic Contribution of IRC Section 1031 Like-Kind Exchanges to the US Economy in 2021," EY, April 29, 2021.

[iv]Bradley T. Borden, Tax-Free Swaps: Using Section 1031 Like-Kind Exchanges to Preserve Investment Net Worth (Nuts & Bolts Series), DNA Press.

[v]Keith A. Wood, "2024 Federal Income Tax Update Part II," Mondaq. com, January 8, 2025.

[vi]Nicole Goodkind, "America Has Lost Half Its Public Companies Since the 1990s. Here's Why," CNN, June 9, 2023.

[vii]"The Golden Age of Multifamily," Linneman Associates, LLC, 2022 (the "Linneman Report").

[viii]Bryan Mick, Mick & Associates.

[ix]"The Total Economic Impact of Capital Square's Opportunity Zone Developments," FTI Consulting, February 2025.

[x]Nicole Funari, "Nareit Research Estimates 145 Million Americans Invested in REITs," Nareit, November 2, 2020.

[xi]"REITs by the Numbers," Nareit, https://www.reit.com/data-re search/data/reits-numbers – Accessed March 2025.

[xii]ibid.

[xiii]"Annual Index Values & Returns: Annual Returns by Property Sector and Subsector: 1994 – 2023," Nareit, 2024.

[xiv]"The Golden Age of Multifamily," Linneman Associates, LLC, 2022 (the "Linneman Report").

[xv]"REITs Own 575,000 Properties in the U.S." Nareit, November 3, 2023.

[xvi]"Annual Index Values & Returns: Annual Returns by Property Sector and Subsector: 1994 – 2023," Nareit, 2024.

[xvii]"REITs by the Numbers," Nareit, https://www.reit.com/data-re search/data/reits-numbers – Accessed March 2025.